Memories Are Made O

Navy Days 1954 to 1966

J N Ash

Index

Memories Are Made Of This

Reveille	Page 3
H.M.S. Ganges	Page 5
H.M.S. Woodbridge Haven	Page 27
H.M.S. Dundas	Page 49
H.M.S. Yarnton	Page 55
H.M.S. Cavalier	Page 59
H.M.S. President	Page 87
H.M.S. Phoenicia	Page 93
H.M.S. Murray	Page 101
H.M.S. President	Page 105
Reflections	Page 114
Last Post	Page 115
Appendix	Page 117

Acknowledgments

My thanks and appreciation to the following:

PETER STUDD	for the Mess Mate & Leisure photographs,	Page 18
GODFREY DYKES,	for the Fleet Anchorage photographs,	Page 32
'ANDY',	for the author of the book 'Make A Signal',	Page 54
BARRY ELTON /GEORGE FRASER	for the Stoker Photographs & names,	Page 74
GEORGE FRASER	for the Cavalier Crew photograph,	Page 83
JUDITH YOUNG	for the NATO badge photograph	Page 98
'ROBBIE BURNS',	for the Ships Badge for HMS Murray,	Page 100
'SARLAD',	for the photographs of HMS Cavalier (Rtd),	Page 120
CHATHAM DOCKYARD	for a wonderful day out	Page 126
CREW OF RUM RATION,	for the contents of the Naval Humour page,	Page 129
P ROGERS	for the Cover Photograph.	

Dedication

**For The Grandchildren
Ben, Matthew & Emmie-Mae.
And The Great Grandchildren
Arlee & Archie.**

'The generations of living things pass in a short time and, like Runners, hand on the torch of life'
Lucretius

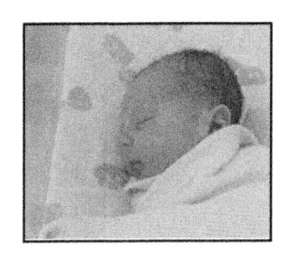

On Valentines day 2005, at the age of 66, I was blessed with the birth of a grand daughter and, by 2015, my eldest Grandson had blessed me with a Great grand daughter and a Great grand son. Realising that I would probably have crossed over the bar before they had grown up and married, I decided to compile a written record of my early life for the grand children. I would not. by any stretch of the imagination. consider it to be an autobiography, but rather something more akin to a signed confession which, as it stands, I doubt will endow me with total absolution but, as they say in Tescos, 'Every little helps'.

And, although written with the grand children in mind, may be of some interest to my contemporaries of the time, hence this book.

Everything I have written, except for facts from photographs or written evidence, has been based on memories, and even these at times can be deceptive. And, although what to one person may be rain, to another may be drizzle and, to a third, a downpour, I have tried to be as accurate and honest as one can be. And, if I have made any glaring errors, please feel free to pen your own amendments - I will be in no position to sue. If, on the other hand, I have missed something which others remember, then it was due to an oversight and failing memory on my part and in no way have I tried to hide something.

Dedicated then to all those paragons who create and maintain our Naval web sites and heritage. If it was still available, I would invite everyone of you round for 'Sippers'.

So, in a light hearted manner, and with a total disregard for Political Correctness, (and before the Tablets wear off), let's publish and be damned. Welcome aboard.

John N Ash, (AKA Jerry Hatrick) Leading Radio Operator.

Duty calls.

Memories Are Made Of This

HMS Ganges

1954 - 1956

'Give a Wise Man instruction and he will be wiser'
Proverbs 9, Verse 9

September 7th 1954

I really have been looking forward to writing this section. I fervently hope that I can do it justice and, that what up to now has been a rather bald and unspectacular narrative, will now become a little more interesting. I should also point out that, as with anything else in this life, in the Navy there were both good and bad times, but overall I loved it and would do the same again. I am still subject to the Official Secrets Act, but I will try to get away with as much as I can.

It was September 7th, 1954 - another date that will forever remain in my memory. I had travelled by train to Ipswich where I and several others were picked up by coach and taken to HMS Ganges, which instead of being a real ship, as I had imagined, was a massive shore establishment. However, instead of going through the main gate we were diverted to a small establishment outside called The Annexe, and this would be home for the next four sunny and warm weeks.

The Annexe consisted of a square parade ground, surrounded on three sides with long mess huts, (dormitories), and on the fourth side a large dinning hall. To one side of the parade ground was a mast flying the White Ensign which filled me with pride. It was late afternoon or early evening when we were taken to the dinning hall for a meal. After that we were allocated to a dormitory with our own bed and locker.

What impressed me most was that. every time we were spoken to by an Instructor. it was always "Now Gentlemen if you will." - I had never been called that before.

Bed and lights out were at Nine and, as I laid in my new surroundings with a full stomach, I felt extremely comfortable and happy - and that feeling lasted all of six hours!

At exactly three in the morning all the lights came on and a giant size Petty Officer picked up a big metal dustbin and bowled it all the way down the Mess between the beds and, with a shout of 'Get out of those sacks', we were all up and on our feet.

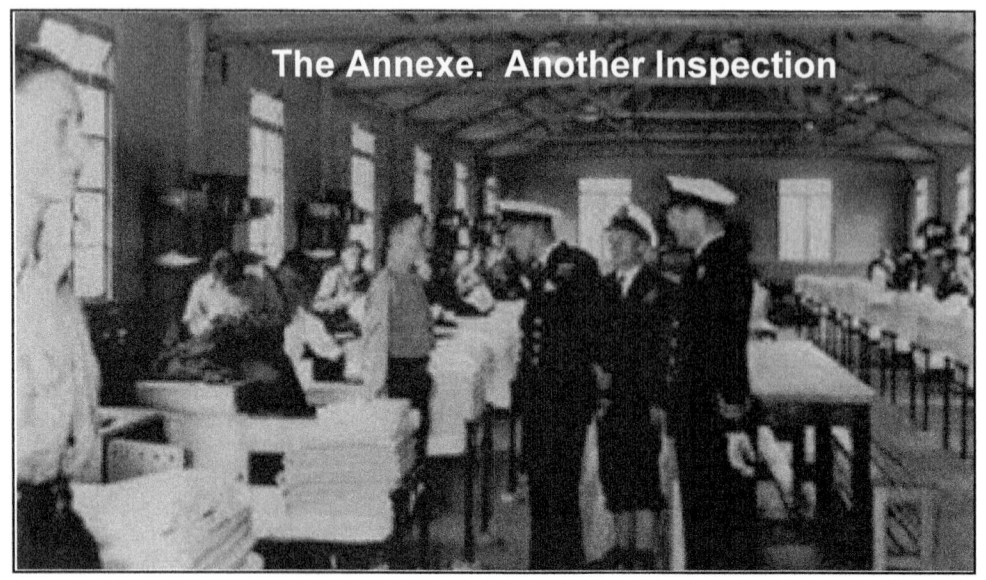

The Annexe. Another Inspection

Initial Pep Talk

We seemed to spend all that day, right up to lights out, running here and there being kitted out, having haircuts marking your name on all your pieces of kit etc etc. On the other hand, we stopped at seven in the morning for a thirty minute cooked breakfast, at ten we had a sticky bun and a cup of thick, sweet chocolate called Kye. At twelve you had one hour for a cooked lunch, tea was at four and then a cooked supper at six. I could not believe it, I had *never* had four meals in one day. We *were* well fed, and throughout my time the food was good, but I did not realise how good until I started eating in a few Restaurants. On the day I joined, my Navy record shows that I was five feet two and weighed seven and a half stone. When I left some twenty months later I was five feet nine and weighed ten and a half stone.

The next day we started to learn how to march, square bashing. Before we started we were lined up to face a giant Petty Officer who gave us a little pep talk which went something like this;

"You are now part of Her Majesty's Royal Navy and, as such, you are now part of the elite".
(Elite, I liked that), (long pause and then),
"If you wish to progress, there are only two things you have to remember".
(Only two things , I liked that),
"One, (long pause), if it moves, you salute and call it sir", (Salute, I could do that).
"And two", (long pause), "If it doesn't move, (long pause), you paint it!".

So the next four weeks were mainly square bashing and learning different manoeuvres to various commands. It may sound boring but, as twenty odd kids started to work and move together as a single entity, it gave you a sense of pride and possibility.

Once a week we had to complete a cross country run and there were two lads in my group who could not complete the course due to asthma. In fairness to the Navy, they put all their medical resources behind these two boys to see if there was anything that could be done for them. Unfortunately there was not, and they were consequently discharged. This was my first experience of how the Navy tried to look after its own, and this would not be my only experience.

Boxing Certificate

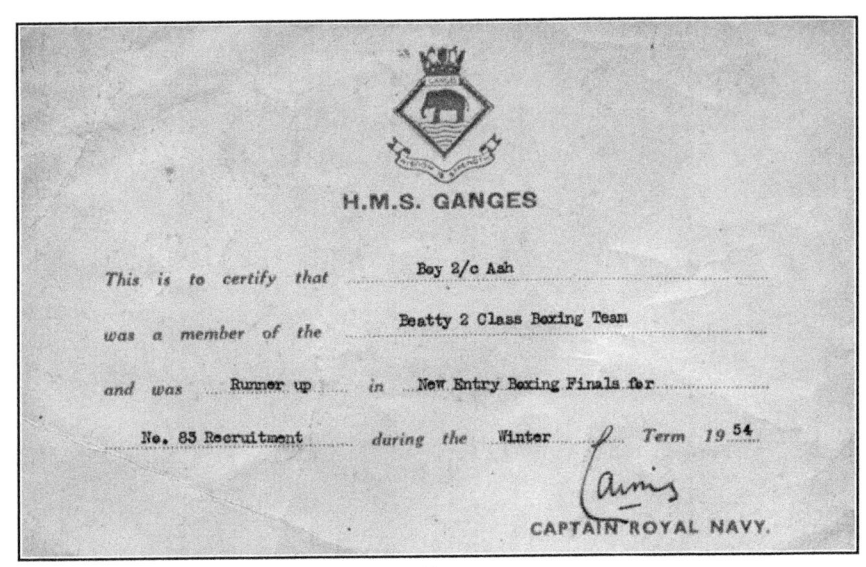

H.M.S. GANGES

This is to certify that Boy 2/c Ash
was a member of the Beatty 2 Class Boxing Team
and was Runner up in New Entry Boxing Finals for
No. 83 Recruitment during the Winter Term 19 54

CAPTAIN ROYAL NAVY.

Selection Processing

During the second weeks training, we were bussed into a Abattoir in Ipswich, and entered the Abattoir via the same entrance as the Pigs going to slaughter. From there we followed the whole process through to where the meat and sausages were being packed for distribution. I think this was the Navy way of finding out how much blood, snot and gore we as individuals could take - subtle eh? Anyway, by some strange coincidence, the following morning we had sausages for breakfast, and I was amazed how many did not get eaten, I think I had three helpings. By now I had realised that besides the basic training, there was also a secretive selection process taking place.

This was confirmed when were told about the Boxing. Over the next three weeks there would be a three, one minute round boxing match once a week, and the winners in the first week would go on to face one another the following week. My first match was with a lad who weighed the same as myself but was much shorter, and all I had to do was hold out my fist and let him run on to it. Second match we were both evenly matched and I just about won. On the final match we were again both evenly matched but I lost. However I did get a Boxing certificate with which I was very pleased. And I concluded that this little excise was to determine if we had enough stomach to knock ten barrels of crap out of one of our mates.

On our third week we had our Sex Lecture. Now, I do not know what they teach the youngsters in school today, but I hope it was nothing like the lesson we had. It was a whole hour taken up by just about every sexual disease under the sun, with grotesque pictures of the consequences of these diseases. I remember that afterwards a couple of my mates who had been with me at the abattoir were sick, and, as for me, I was fifteen and a half at the time, and I did not have sex until I was seventeen - and then rather reluctantly.

Who would have thought that four weeks ago we were on the last of our summer school holidays with few and far between employment prospects, and now here we were on the payroll of Her Majesty The Queen. I think that it was also the first time in my life that I went to bed without feeling hungry.

End of Training and the Annexe for No. 85 Recruitment, October 1954

Morse And Swimming Tests

During the same week we were taken into the dinning hall and had to learn in fifteen minutes three characters from the Morse code. These characters were then played back at random to us for about another fifteen minutes, and we had to write down what they were. Two days later I was informed that I could go on the Telegraphist course when I was drafted to the Main Establishment. I guessed that I had passed another selection process.

During the fourth week we were told that we would be going to the indoor swimming pool in the Main Establishment. There we would be required to put on a white cotton uniform, shout out our name, jump off the top diving board, swim to the side and get out. Great! I had never been swimming fully dressed, and I intended to have some fun. The pool was big with six lanes and high diving boards. Around the pool were several Physical Instructors carrying long poles with a big hook on the end. As I stood watching it became obvious that some of my mates could not swim, and their inadequacies and reluctance showed. I also noticed that after each jump the Instructors would make notes in a small pad they were carrying. I was going to give them something to write home about.

I made sure that I was the last to go and reluctantly climbed to the top board and then gingerly peeked over the edge as an Instructor shouted "I told you to jump. Jump!"., but instead I turned around and started walking back down the board and, as I noticed the instructors coming towards the board, I shouted out "Ash", I took a run, leaped off the end and did a perfect bum first bomb with my knees firmly held under my chin - what a splash. I then let myself sink to the bottom and swam under water to the shallow end. At the shallow end wall, still under water, I turned quickly, kicked off and swam back to the deep end. When I surfaced I had four instructors with poles at the ready glaring at me, so I coughed and spluttered and said, "Sorry sir, I got a bit lost". (When ever you tell a flagrant lie like the one I had just told, it was *always* taken in good humour). However, when I got out, a glaring Instructor said to me "Ash, I've made a note of your name". I hoped that he had, and I would perform a similar stunt later in my Naval career.

Annexe trainees selected to become Telegraphists (Radio Operators).

Into The Main Establishment

The selection processes over the past four weeks had reduced the number of new entrants by about five, and it was now our turn to march smartly over to the Main Establishment and start our proper training. I felt really proud as we went through the main gate in a column of three. The tradition at this time was for the other thousand trainees in the Establishment to line the route and cheer/jeer us in. Imagine my pride when I heard one of them say, "They are a tough looking bunch", but when his mate replied, "Well, they will have to be, wont they?", I was not quite so sure.

Now, as the latest entry, you were referred to as a "Nozzer", and a "Nozzer" you remained until the next lot entered in four weeks time. And you could tell a Nozzer a mile away. Everyone else's work uniform was faded from washing whereas a Nozzer's clothes were still a deep Navy blue

Did I mention money and Pay Days? We were paid once a fortnight on a Wednesday. For the first twelve months I was paid five shillings, (25p), a fortnight rising to seven shillings and sixpence, (37.5p), thereafter. Actually we earned a little more than that, but the remainder was kept back so that we could purchase replacements for worn out pieces of uniform.

One morning during the first month, our Instructor called out about a dozen names including mine. He then instructed us to go to the swimming pool and report to the duty Physical Training Instructor for swimming lessons. Swimming? - Yes. Lessons? - I could not believe it! It looked as though my skylarking had backfired. When we got to the pool, the Instructor called out "Ash. Is Ash here?". I went up to him and said that I was Ash. He looked up and down my five feet two frame, looked at his notes, scratched his head and said "Come with me". He took me to the left hand lane of the pool and, while all the others were standing on the side watching, he told me to get into the water and swim to the far end as fast as I could. I was not sure so I asked whether he wanted me to jump in and swim or dive and go for it.

He said he just wanted me to get to the other end as fast as I could, and flashed the stop watch in his hand. As soon as he said "Go" I dived in with feet paddling the air before I hit the water, and I knew I that could swim the whole length without taking a breath.

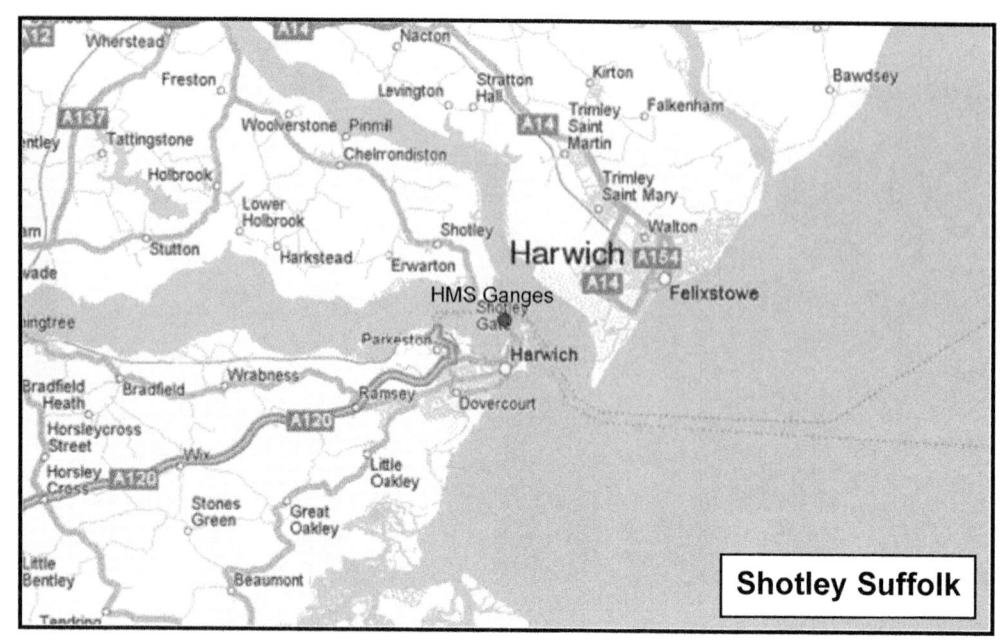

Shotley Suffolk

My First Leave

At the other end of the pool I saw him check the watch and write some notes. He then said to me that in two weeks time a swimming team would be going to Ipswich for a competition Gala. He wanted me as a reserve with a chance to swim, would I like to go. After only four weeks I was being *asked* to swim for the Navy, I could not wait to go, and I did swim - Porchester, eat your heart out.

I think it was during the first month that I had a Sunday visit from Joan and two of the lads from school. It was great to see her and the chaps, but I think that both Joan and I knew then that we were now in different worlds, and for us this would be the last time that we would see each other.

I really liked Joan, and I always had the impression that Joan did not feel properly dressed until she was on the arm of her boyfriend, and for me that had been great but, now, no longer possible.

In December we were given three weeks leave to cover the Christmas period and new year, it was the worse Christmas I can remember.

I arrived home excited and proud in my uniform but everything had changed. My bicycle had gone, my Sunday School prize books had vanished and so had my civilian clothes.

I felt like a stranger in my own home, and I think I then realised that there was nothing here for me, and the Navy was where I needed to be. The three weeks seemed to drag, and I think I spent most of the time in the local cinema watching the same film.

That night when I got back to Shotley, I cried myself to sleep hoping none of my mates could hear me.

View from the top of the mast

Felixstowe on the left — Harwich on the right

The Mess Routine

Mess ready for inspection, sir.

Kit ready for inspection, sir.

Saturday mornings were spent cleaning and getting the Mess ready for the Divisional Officer's Inspection at noon.

Our Divisional Officer's wife would bake a cake for the best Mess and, for reasons which I am not prepared to go into, we always tried to come second.

A Kit Inspection was held on every other Wednesday morning by the Divisional officer who, invariably, gave the kit a casual glance, muttered something like 'Good, good' and passed on.

However, if his deputy carried out the Inspections, then you knew you were going to have problems. He would enter with a cane in his hand, prod it into a pair of your underpants, hold the whole lot up to the light, and then flick the pants over his shoulder. By the time he had finished, the Mess deck floor was strewn with underwear and other items of kit, and you couldn't believe the distance some of your items had travelled.

And his parting remark was always something like, 'Excellent, keep up the good work'.

All kit had to marked with your name, and all items of kit had to be stored in your locker with the name on each item of kit visible, and the locker doors had to remain in the open position. This ensured that you could not hide any illicit items, and completely eliminated theft. The Navy knew what it was doing.

Locker ready for inspection, sir.

Telegraphist Training

By the start of the 1955 term, I had a pretty good idea of how the Radio Operators course would pan out, and why it took some eighteen months to complete.

First of all It took three or four months just to learn the Morse Code. The next obstacle was the increasing speeds at which you had to be able to read the code. The difference between ten words per minute and twelve may not sound much but, with each increase in speed, you had a barrier to get over. Our instructors had all gone through these phases and were a great help.

Our instructor, Chief Petty Officer Hotchkiss, had what to day would be called 'A Cunning Plan'. If we were training at twelve words a minute, he would, before the next exam, slowly speed it up to thirteen, so the exam speeds always seemed slower.

In the eighteen months training we had to be 95% accurate at 22 WPM to pass out. However, once you had reached 20 WPM the barriers disappeared and 25 WPM with a typewriter was quite feasible.

Did I mention a typewriter? Well that was also part of the course - a full twelve month Pitmans typing course, with a pass of 95% accuracy and 40 WPM.

With the later arrival of computers and keyboards, this little sideline well and truly set me up. Six months into the course and you started Cryptography and Radio Theory - I loved it and still have my Radio Theory notebook. Although by now I already knew roughly how my old Crystal Set had worked, I was now in a position to explain how it worked. But why the six month wait?

Well, during my first term I had not only been told about the Telegraphist course, but had also been informed that we would undergo eighteen months of extra schooling, and that there would be two exams to pass Educational Test 1 (ET1) and ET2. ET2 allowed you to stay in the Navy but, if you wanted Promotion, you had to have ET1. - I knew I should have read the small print.

Typical Morse Code Training

Keyboard Training

Now, the thought of having to live through eighteen months of my Beethoven secondary school type education filled me with gloom, and the idea that I had to pass two exams did not help. And when I heard that the first lesson was going to be what sounded like Trigonometry, I just died. But it was nothing like I had imagined. The Navy did not call it Trigonometry, they called it *Navigation* and, instead of a sheet of paper, we were given real Admiralty charts and all the Chart navigation instruments. We were taught how to calculate course and speed against wind and tide and plot a course and calculate Time of Arrival. And it got even better.

For physics we had Magnetism and Electricity which, of course, was the basic knowledge required for the Radio theory course in six months time. However, I did have a minor moan when I saw our first History lesson looming. In school we never got past the Roman period, and no one ever spoke about early twentieth century history.

But this history was different - it was Naval history, Drake, Frobisher, Benbow and Nelson. It was all the subjects that I had previously read about from our local Library. The outcome of this type of education was that I breezed through both exams, and won the Religious Instruction prize.

Besides the above, there was the rifle range, which I loved, and small arms training, physical training, sailing, cinema, a massive mast to climb and just about every sport imaginable. I had chosen swimming and, for two afternoons each week, I had the pool to myself with my Trainer 'Sharky' Ward. He was the one that had threateningly taken my name on my first visit to the pool, but he was a great Instructor and coach.

If my secondary education had been my local Library and the museums, then the Navy education was the icing on the cake, and it set me in good stead for the remainder of my life.

Typical Typewriter Training

HMS Ganges 1954 - 1956   Memories Are Made Of This

Cutter Crew

15

HMS Ganges 1954 - 1956   Memories Are Made Of This

A Typical Day

Sticks And Carrots

Before I leave this section, I would like to relate a couple of incidents that I witnessed while in training, which might give some idea as to the flavour of the Navy at that time.

During the winter term of 1955, one of the Trainees decided to abscond during the night.

I ought to explain that the establishment was bordered on two sides by two rivers, in front were the rivers estuaries with Harwich on the far side.

And, as can be seen from the map, there was only one route out, and that was the single nine mile Road to Ipswich railway station.

It is also worth mentioning that the winters in Suffolk can be quite mean. This lad had obviously never read a Paul Brickhill book. Anyway, he was only out for about four hours when the Police brought him back half frozen and handed him over.

The Navy wrapped him in blankets, took him to the galley, where it was warm, fed him and, when a Doctor had determined that he was alright, sent him back to his bed.

For an offence of this magnitude, the disciplinary proceedings would take place on the Parade Ground in front of everyone.

The punishment in this case was a caning, and he was duly led off. Four weeks later, on the same Parade Ground in front of everyone, he was promoted to a Leading Boy, (the equivalent of a school Prefect).

This was the Navy way of making sure that Naval Discipline had been satisfied and, at the same time, openly encouraging a sense of adventure and spirit.

The other incident involved everyone in my Class. . . . .

Telegraphist Exams

Typical Navigation Class

HMS Ganges 1954 - 1956					Memories Are Made Of This

Mess Mates and Leisure Time

Hawke 251 & 252 Class 1955

Gymnasium - Boxing Match

At the Sports ground.

Dress Of The Day

The second incident happened when one of the lads in our Mess fell foul of a Gunnery Instructor. Gunnery Instructors were the backbone of the Navy and probably the most disciplined, toughest and smartest men in the Service. (When I say smartest, I am talking about their uniforms rather than their intelligence. The latter invariably consisted of three things only; Her Majesty, Gawd bless 'er, England expects etc, and Engage the enemy more closely). Anyway, instead of having a go at the lad, he made the whole class fall in outside the mess. At the time we were all dressed in our sports gear. He then looked at his watch and said, "You have two minutes in which to go back inside, change into Overalls and fall in outside. Go!".

With a rush and flurry of bodies, within two minutes we were all fallen in outside wearing our overalls, wondering what dirty job he had in mind for us - anything except sweeping the parade ground with a toothbrush. He then looked at his watch and said "You have got two minutes in which to go back inside and get changed into your working gear, and fall in outside. Go!". Once we had all got back inside it became obvious to all of us that he was going to get us to change into every item of uniform we had so that our lockers would look a real jumble.

We all decided that, as we had nothing to lose, to put on every item of kit that we had and, in a little more than two minutes, we all fell in again looking like walking wardrobes. When he saw us his face was one of sheer disbelief and, after what seemed to be an age of silence, his face broke into a grin and he said "Alright lads, good effort. I admire your spirit, dismiss". We all had a bit of a laugh about it afterwards and, in this case, we thought that both sides could claim a victory.

In March 1956 I passed out of Ganges as a very proud Junior Telegraphist ready in all respects for sea. It was not the end of my training, and for the next year I would be learning how to operate communications receivers, transmitters and a cryptographic machine - but this time on a real ship.

My first ship was HMS Woodbridge Haven, a wartime Frigate based in Malta, and I was to fly out to Malta on the 30th of March. I was issued with my Tropical Kit and flew from Blackbushe Airport, courtesy of Eagle Airways who, incidentally, served an excellent Minestrone soup - nothing else, just Minestrone soup.

The next generation of Radio Operators
X

HMS Ganges 1954 - 1956   Memories Are Made Of This

Manning the Mast

This was before we had the Health & Safety Risk Assessment Forms

And Finally . . .

Sunday Morning Divisions

End of Telegraphist Training

School Education Certificate

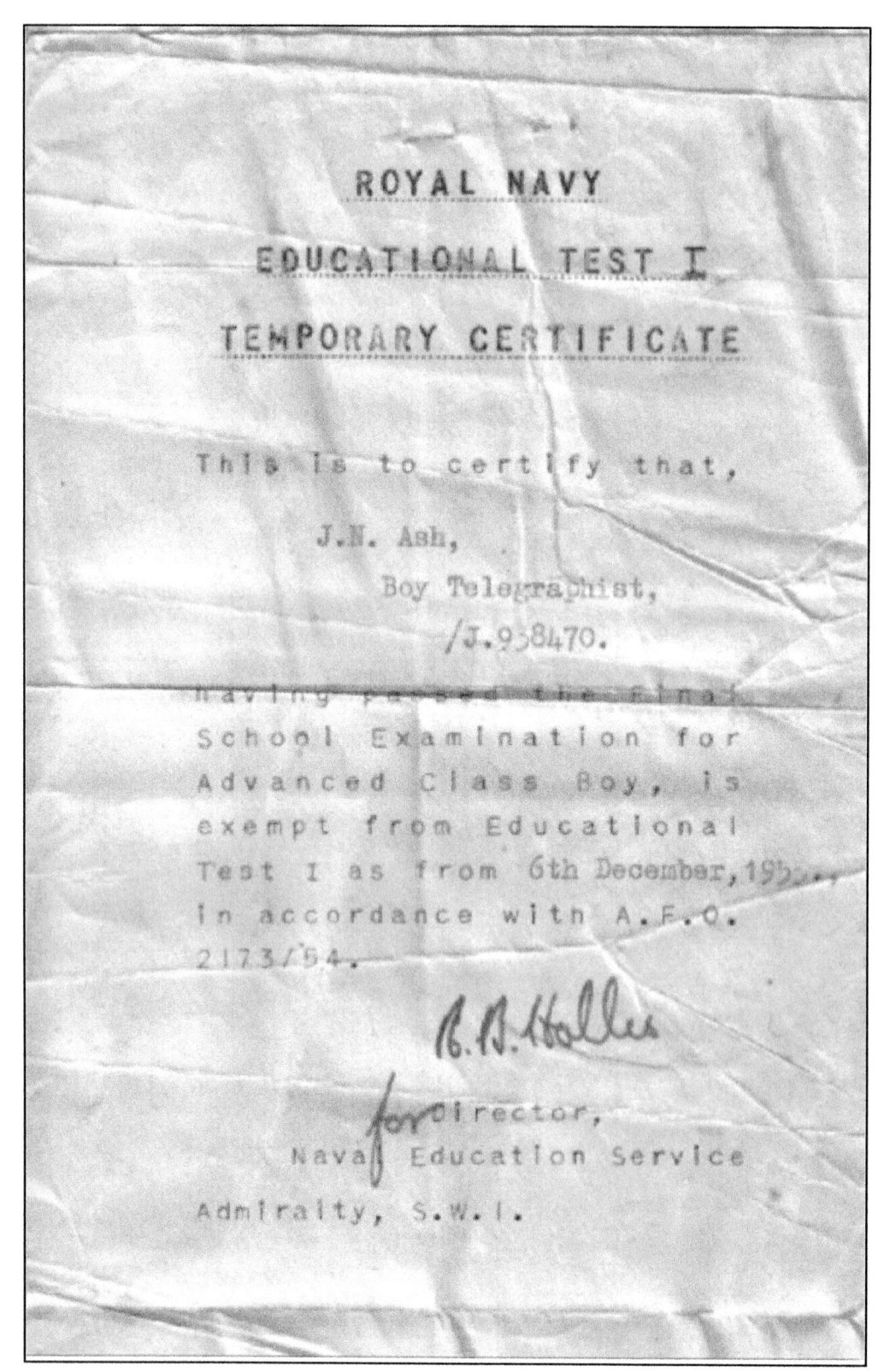

> ROYAL NAVY
>
> EDUCATIONAL TEST I
>
> TEMPORARY CERTIFICATE
>
> This is to certify that,
>
> J.N. Ash,
> Boy Telegraphist,
> /J.958470.
>
> having passed the final School Examination for Advanced Class Boy, is exempt from Educational Test I as from 6th December, 195..., in accordance with A.F.O. 2173/54.
>
> *B.B. Holles*
>
> for Director,
> Naval Education Service
> Admiralty, S.W.1.

HMS Ganges 1954 - 1956   Memories Are Made Of This

End of Training

Future Signalmen and Telegraphists

Passing Out Guard Duty

HMS Ganges 1954 - 1956   Memories Are Made Of This

A trip down memory lane

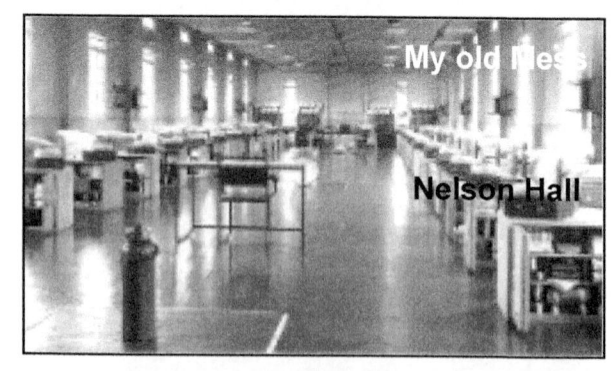

Stand Easy

Whilst in Ganges, the Instructors would often relate some of their Navy experiences and war time stories, with the odd derogatory remark aimed at either the American or Italian Navies. This is a war time story I heard from one of the Instructors. It was aimed at the American Navy and may well be fiction.

Apparently a task force of American ships, headed by an Aircraft Carrier, were steaming up the English Channel at dusk, headed for Plymouth.

The Admiral in charge of the task force was on the bridge of the Carrier when an English voice came over the radio saying, "Unknown ships, you are on a collision course with me. Please turn fifteen degrees to the south, over".

A furious Admiral picked up the microphone and balled at the unknown voice, "I suggest that you turn fifteen degrees to the north. Out".

Back came the voice saying, "I really must insist that you turn fifteen degrees to the south".

The Admiral bawled into the microphone, "This is the USS _____, the second largest Aircraft Carrier in the world, accompanied by two Cruisers and five Destroyers, and I will take any action necessary to protect my vessels. And who the hell are you anyway?".

Back came the voice, "This is the Eddystone Lighthouse, over".

Now it's time to fly to the sunny Med and my first ship. . . . .

Now, at the risk of infringing the Official Secrets Act, I place in the public domain one of the Navy's best kept secrets, the recipe for Kye.

Try making navy-style hot chocolate ('Kye').

This recipe is enough for two people (in most cases).

1. Break a small bar of plain dark chocolate into pieces.
2. Place pieces in a saucepan with one mug of hot Water.
3. Heat up until the chocolate has melted.
4. Add one tin of condensed milk.
5. Bring to the boil and serve in mugs.
6. Add copious amounts of sugar to taste.

When out at sea, on look-out watch,
The hours pass slowly by,
But maybe someone brings to me
A mug of steaming kye.

What happened to the slim, fresh-faced young boy who left here 12 weeks ago?

Memories Are Made Of This

HMS Woodbridge Haven

1956 - 1957

'Every man thinks meanly of himself for not having been at sea'
Dr Samuel Johnson

First Ship

The two things I noticed when I arrived in Malta was that it was hot and that, when I arrived at the quay side in Sliema Creek, there was no HMS Woodbridge Haven - she had sailed a couple of days earlier for a good will trip to Beirut.

So, for the first two weeks I was transferred to two Minesweepers, HMS Essington & HMS Hickleton. (I flip flopped between the two, depending on which one required painting). I loved the small ships, the food was good, the routine was good, and the Radio Office was how I imagined one would be. They only carried one Radio Operator and he showed me how to use the equipment. Two days onboard and Essington went to sea on a short mine sweeping exercise. I stood on the deck as we sailed past a sunken World War 2 merchant vessel, and out of Grand Harbour feeling very proud but, as soon as we got past the Breakwater, I felt queasy and soon became very sea sick. I was to suffer from sea sickness for the next two years, it was sheer unadulterated purgatory and I hated it.

Once on board the 'WooHa' as she was affectionately known, I was lodged in the Juniors mess with my own hammock space and about ten other various juniors. In charge was a Leading Seaman who gave us physical training at six each morning, kept us on our toes and, at the same time, kept us out of trouble. He was a wealth of information. As at Ganges, lights out for us was at nine

The Wireless office was small, cramped and full of equipment. I have forgotten the name of the Petty Officer Telegraphist, (POTS), but he was a great man and taught me a lot, and every day I would take part in some kind of operating exercise.

One of the exercises was a NATO Test Message. I was allowed to pick any NATO addressee I fancied, load up a transmitter and try to contact a NATO radio station - with me it was always Rome. The message said that this is a NATO Test Message, report time of receipt. It was a method of testing the communication systems, and I always looked out for the reply.

After about a month or two, I was introduced to the cryptographic machine. It was on a desk top covered by a wooden hinged lid and, I do not think that I will be giving too much away when I say that it was big, black and looked quite complicated. (Later in life when I saw a German wartime Enigma machine, I was struck by how similar it looked to ours, and it occurred to me that somehow we had got hold of one of the German Enigma machines and copied it). I loved cryptography. As you typed, the plain text would start to appear on a paper tape as if by magic. The first couple of words would tell you if it was Confidential, Secret or Top Secret. At that time, I did not see many of the latter two, but in six months time that was all I would be seeing.

HMS Essington in Sliema Creek, Malta

Communications Mess

Our Diceoh Man

Sliema Creek

"Diceoh!"

Minesweeper's Diceoh Man

Dghajsas, pronounced Dice-oh, were a very popular form of transport, and could be found just about anywhere along the Creeks and shores of Malta. They were highly decorated in bold colours, and kept scrupulously clean by their proud owners.

With our Minesweepers tied to buoys in the centre of Sliema Creek, the flotilla's Dghajsa man became an important member of the team, and was kept continuously busy either ferrying from ship to shore and back, or running errands to the local Bars for additional cold drinks.

Our Dghajsa man, pictured above, was always there when ever you wanted him, and nothing was ever too much trouble. He was very popular with all of the Minesweeper's crews and, for most part, he was treated as a member of the ships Company.

At the top of the Baracca lift in Valletta, are the Barakka Gardens with great views across Grand Harbour. The Gardens contain a small water feature - the Maltese equivalent of one of the Trafalgar Square fountains.

There was a story circulating at the time that, late one night, a Royal Marine in full Mess Dress uniform and regalia, was discovered standing knee deep in the middle of the fountain, drunk as a Lord, waving a half empty bottle of Marsavin in the air, and calling out, "Diceoh, Diceoh".

Barakka Garden Fountain

Life At Sea

HMS Woodbridge Haven and the 104th and 108th minesweeping squadrons, all based in Malta at that time, on manoeuvres prior to the Suez conflict.

WooHa with her flock the 104th & 108th Minesweeping Squadron

*"Do You Hear there.
Maths class will take place in the Junior's Mess in 2+2+1 minutes time"*

Malta

The 'WooHa' was the support ship for, and In charge of, all the Minesweepers based in Sliema Creek and, although they would go to sea and exercise on a regular basis, we tended to stay tied up at our berth on Manoel Island , and sea sickness was not a problem at this time. I was beginning to love Malta. The bus services into Valletta were frequent and cheap, and I loved the milling crowds that would gather of an evening in Kingsway, Valletta's main thorough fare.

Running parallel and next to Kingsway is Strait street or, as we used to call it, 'The Gut'. It was one long, narrow street of continuous Bars, bright lights, loud music and obese women - but I liked it. There were two bars which I preferred to frequent. The first was the Egyptian Queen, the only Bar with a live band, if you can call a saxophone player and a drummer a band. The other Bar, and probably my favourite, was Dirty Dick's and, contrary to it's name, it was quite respectable and the owner, whose name *was* Richard, made the best cocktails in Malta. The reason why it was called Dirty Dick's is because each time you paid for a drink, Richard would give you a small card with some filthy innuendo printed on it. I used to have quite a collection. There was also a restaurant in the Gut called Ben Marl's, where the owner would stand outside shouting 'Big eats, boys'. Fortunately, the emanating smell put me off, and I never got to sample his gastronomic delights.

Just outside Valletta is Florianna and, tucked away between some shops, was a restaurant called Chez Vency which, at the time, was probably the best restaurant in Malta. All the Navy lads used to rave about the restaurant's steaks and mixed grills. Remember that this was in the days before we had Curry Houses, and that there was still a meat shortage at home.

Round about late September or early October it was becoming obvious to me that something 'Big' was happening which included the 'WooHa'. Rumours were rife, and I seemed to be spending a lot more time on the cryptographic machine and, instead of working a somewhat nine to five routine, I was now working in twenty four hour watches (shifts). My very first watch was eight p.m. until midnight. I got back to the Juniors mess three hours after lights out to find the Leading Seaman in charge sitting up waiting for me. He had saved some food for me from supper, made sure I was alright and saw me to my hammock before turning in himself.

During October, you could not help but notice the additional warships that were arriving in Malta and the activity over in the dockyards and, when we took on board a team of Navy Divers, and two more Radio Operators who were about to leave the Navy and who insisted on being called 'Mister', I *knew* it was going to be big. In late October we sailed for an unknown destination.

Accompanied by our Minesweepers, I could tell from the sun that we were sailing in an easterly direction, but to where? It was about this time that the cryptographic machine started to yield up some of the secrets and, after a couple of days the Captain announced that we were heading for Suez, gave a brief overview of why and what was expected of us. Our task was for our Minesweepers to go in first to clear, and mark, a channel for the ships and landing craft carrying the combined Army and Marine landing force.

The radio signals were coming in fast, in some length and all needed to be decoded and, even if the signal was not for the 'WooHa', it still had to be decoded and passed to the Captain. We now seemed to be working four hours on, four hours off day and night - including the two 'Misters'. Each day as we drew nearer to Port Said there seemed to be more and more ships on the horizon, and the whole fleet was eventually joined by the French Navy. I had read about the D-Day Landings, now I understood how it must have felt - confident but nervous.

Malta - Typical Fleet Anchorages

Lazaretto Creek

The Navy in Malta

Sliema Creek

Suez

Before we arrived, the Radio Supervisor took me to one side and told me that during the operation he wanted me to man the emergency wireless station located in the stern of the ship. He told me to check the equipment regularly, but under no circumstances transmit unless told to do so. And he ended by saying that if the main wireless office "Lost power" it would all be up to me. Realising that "Lost Power" was an euphemism for taking a hit, I felt a little uneasy and wondered what Jack French, my schoolboy hero Telegraphist on the "Amethyst", would have done.

As we approached Port Said, all watertight doors and hatches were closed and battened down, and the ship internally darkened except for the occasional red light. Port said had already been battered and bombed by our aircraft and bombarded by our big ships. It looked a mess. Our Minesweepers had a clear channel plotted in record time, and we and they were then retired to a position about three miles out to sea.

There seemed little resistance, and within three or four days it was all over. The 'WooHa' was ordered into Port Said where we tied up not far from DeLessops statue. Our next task was to support the Diving Team whose job was to tackle the sunken wrecks from the mouth of the canal, whilst the Minesweepers patrolled the shallow waters. While in Port Said we were allowed shore leave and, as we wandered around I was struck by two things, the first was how much damage and destruction had been caused, and secondly, just how friendly the natives were towards us.

After a while the United Nations force seemed to take over, and eventually we, and our flock of Minesweepers, were ordered back to Malta. I could not help thinking that somehow we were leaving with our tails between our legs, and that the Navy had done something wrong. I certainly did not feel like a conquering hero, and to some extent I think I felt slightly ashamed. I could not explain why, but the perception remained with me until my arrival back in England some months later.

When we arrived back in Malta and tied up in Sliema Creek, I got the distinct feeling that, as a Navy, we had nothing to do. I think I was feeling a little demoralised and depressed. But on the other hand, it was the official start of the 'Rock 'n Roll' era, and I was becoming a very competent Junior Telegraphist, with some sea time under my belt. It was also my first Christmas on board a ship.

Comment on our withdrawal

"Heroes of Sinai and Suez! The enemy is on the run—don't shoot until you see the white of their BACKS!"

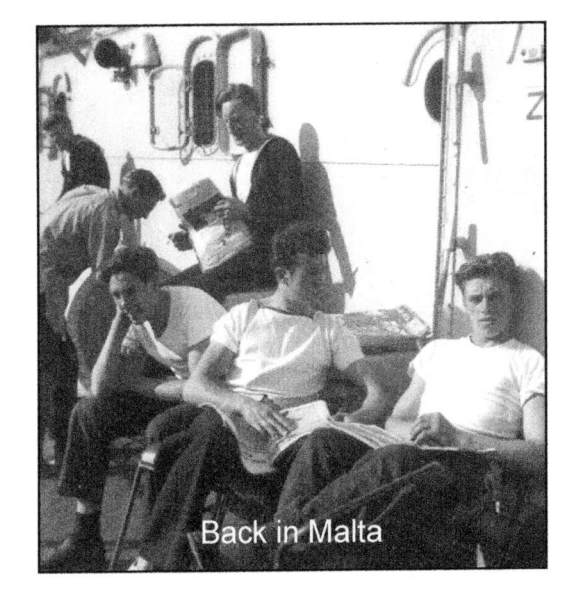

Back in Malta

Suez

Port Said at Dawn November 6th 1956

At the time, we were unaware that the Suez Crisis was causing riots in the streets back home, and that the news media had called it a 'Fiasco'. I think that we were possibly subject to a Home news blackout in order to keep up morale.

This was referred to as being given the 'Mushroom Treatment' - that is when you are kept in the dark and fed on bullshit.

This was not the Navy way of doing things, and I still believe the news blackout originated with our Politicians of the time.

Attack Force

London

HMS Woodbridge Haven 1956 - 1957　　　　　　　　　　　　　　　Memories Are Made Of This

Suez

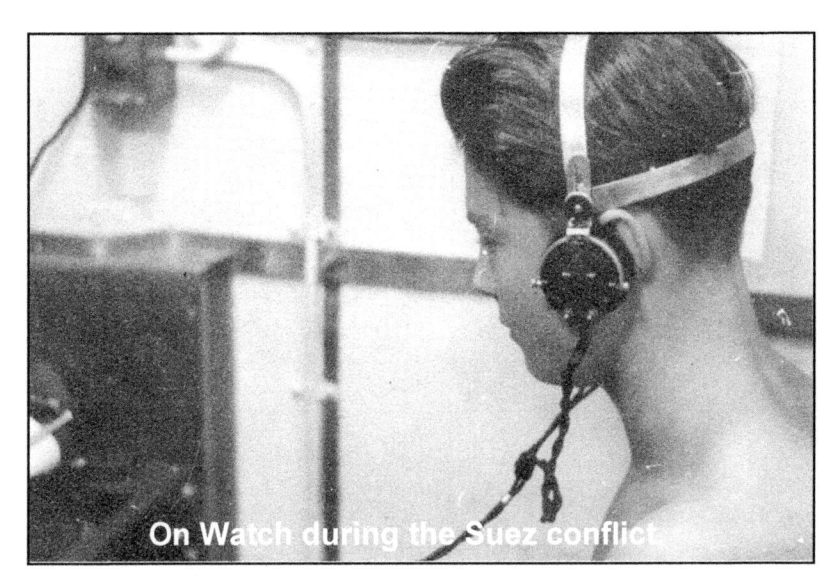

On Watch during the Suez conflict.

'DeLessops' Statue.

When I look back on this period of my life, I still find it a little amusing that aged seventeen I, and my contemporaries, were eligible to participate in the Suez conflict but, at the same time, our Politicians considered us to be too young to either vote or have a drink in a Pub.

Diving team

Typical Canal block ship.

Street Damage

U.N. takeover.

Aftermath

HMS Woodbridge Haven 1956 - 1957　　　　　　　　　　Memories Are Made Of This

Suez Album

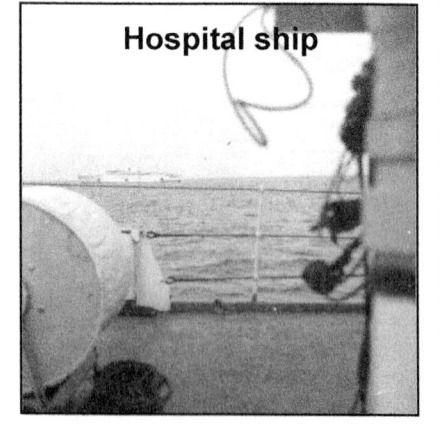

- CMS, 'WooHa' & Meon
- Port Said from the sea
- Port Said berth
- Canal block ships
- Hospital ship
- POW camp
- UN Takeover
- Withdrawal

First Christmas Onboard

Sometime prior to Suez, a girl called Vicki, who I knew from Chertsey and whose parents were friends of my parents, had started writing to me and, as we corresponded we became quite friendly with each other, and I looked forward to her letters.

Just before we sailed from Malta for Suez, Vicki had written a letter which hinted of something a little more than just friendship but, before I could write back, all outgoing mail was stopped for security reasons.

So, when we arrived back in Malta, there was a fair bit of mail waiting for us, including another one from Vicki apologising for her last letter. She had thought that, because I had not replied, she had said too much and upset the apple cart.

I wrote back with a long explanation why I had not replied, what we had been doing and that everything was fine. From that point onward, the correspondence moved up a gear.

On the 23 rd of November I was promoted to Ordinary Telegraphist and moved into the Communications Mess.

Christmas on board a ship is full of custom and tradition. The Christmas Pudding has to be stirred by the Captain months in advance and, for Christmas day only, the youngest member of the crew is dressed in the Captain's uniform and is put in charge and what he says goes.

All this was new to me and, with enough booze on board to float a Battleship, I had a good Christmas and my first taste of Rum - and I have loved it ever since.

On January 31 st, having all sobered up to a reasonable level, we sailed on a Good Will trip to Messina in Sicily. And I expect, Dear Reader, that by now you have already calculated that I was seventeen, and that this must be where I lose my innocence.

Correct. But, if you are a Barbara Cartland fan or have a similar leaning, you may, (he wrote hopefully), wish to skip this next bit - it's gross, but I still tend to think of it as my first brief romantic interlude.

Mail in

Mail out

Innocence Lost

"Deeps" and Me (Before)

My mate 'Deeps' Deeprose and I were out sightseeing around Messina taking in the civic architecture and Sicilian culture, when it became quite obvious from all the "Come Hither's" we were getting that we were in the middle of the Brothel zone.

After a lengthy, futile discussion, and a pack of lies about how long it had been since we had last been with a girl, and having then convinced ourselves that we were both just about due again, in we went - lambs to the slaughter, and I've seen more hygiene and better looking bodies in an Ipswich Abattoir

However, we were now in and I could think of no way of backing out so, in the best of British traditions, and with a stiff upper lip (only), I went for it.

I was offered a choice of *two* women, but they both looked as bad as each other, and could have been twins. We then had to haggle over the price which was quoted in Lira and, although it seemed a lot money, when you remember there was about two or three million Lira to the pound, I probably ended up paying a couple of bob - but to this day I still feel robbed.

Anyway, she led me into a bedroom and, having removed my trousers and pants, I was taken to a sink in the corner to give, what up till then had been my *private* parts, a thorough scrub, which had the desired effect. What I had not realised was that I had only paid for "Short Time", and the rest is a little bit of a blur.

I was dragged over to the bed, which I noticed was still warm, and then on top of her. I had to keep the rest of my clothes on - including socks and hob nailed boots. She then dragged me back to the sink in the corner, gave me another good scrub and sent me on my way. It could not have taken more than two minutes, and when I got outside, clutching my pants and trousers, there was 'Deeps' already dressed and waiting for me.

Talk about Quick Draw McGraw - it takes me longer to *boil* an egg.

I think for the next fortnight I constantly re-lived the Annexe Sex Lecture nightmare, and I spent all my free time in the showers with a bottle of Dettol, expecting to see something drop off at any moment.

However, (wrote he, rapidly changing the subject), I was still relatively young and, with the Navy and a bottle of Dettol behind me, I was beginning to feel like a man, confident, independent and, with everything still intact, fairly pleased with myself.

HMS Woodbridge Haven 1956 - 1957　　　　　　　　　　　　Memories Are Made Of This

Venice

WooHa arriving in Venice with HMS Birmingham

Venice waterfront

HMS Woodbridge Haven 1956 - 1957 　　　　　Memories Are Made Of This

Italian Trips

Crew Changeover

I had been on the 'WooHa' for nine months but the rest of the crew had spent eighteen months on board and were due to fly home except for those who had their wives with them. For the latter, it was a two and a half year stint. When the new crew arrived I had to get to know everybody all over again, and you could see the character of the ship changing.

The two characters I remember most are "Taff" Evens and Ron Madle. "Taff" was from South Wales and seemed to know Tredegar. We were great pals and went everywhere together. Ron was the new Leading Telegraphist and he was brilliant at his job, a wealth of information and extremely fair minded. On the other hand Ron was also the most undisciplined, laid back and laziest bloke I had yet come across and, to boot, the most physically unfit. Ron could roll a cigarette, and then convince himself that he'd had enough exercise for one week, and retire to his bunk.

Now, I am beginning to feel that I have spent far to long on this section so let me round it off as quickly as I can. In march we sailed to show the flag at Monaco for Grace and Prince Ranier's wedding. And my schoolboy French came in handy as we went sightseeing along the Riviera.

A couple of months later we visited Trapani in Sicily and then Naples. This cruise was quickly followed by a trip to Venice and La Spezia in northern Italy. In La Spezia, I was ashore with two of my mates and a very accommodating Italian Policeman took us to a local brothel in some dingy back street.

The building looked old and dilapidated with peeling paint and when the door was opened by a sixty year old wizened hag, I started to have my doubts, and prayed that this one was not going to be mine. However, inside it was like a marble palace with statues and fountains. We were taken to a room where the hag offered us drinks and told us to wait.

A few minutes later in walked about ten of the most beautiful women I had ever seen, and they were all dressed in fur, feathers, silk and satin. The hag then instructed us to choose - it was difficult, but I settled on a beautiful blonde in her mid to late twenties. Her name was Gincia, and I was in love.

The bedroom was beautiful with silks and satins everywhere, and the obligatory sink in the corner. This time, I made sure I was not paying for Short Time. I was so in love that next day I went straight back and demanded Gincia, and a few minutes later she appeared and greeted me with a beautiful smile and said "Ah, Bambino! Multi benne". I think I will take the memory of her with me to the grave.

Aerial Maintenance

Me, Taff and Ron - It was a hard life at sea

HMS Woodbridge Haven 1956 - 1957   Memories Are Made Of This

Life at sea

Wooha leaving Trapani, Sicily

HMS Woodbridge Haven 1956 - 1957 — Memories Are Made Of This

Monaco

Entering Monte Carlo Harbour, Monaco, for the Ranier's Wedding

Monte Carlo Casino

Grace Kelly
&
Prince Rainier

Monte Carlo

Eze

Italian Border Bazaar

Eze

Cyprus Patrol

In September we were in Cyprus on patrol. There was friction between the Greek and Turkish inhabitants, and our job was to act as a deterrent against merchant ships gun running and bringing in illicit cargoes. At night, we sailed with the ship darkened close into the shore so that our silhouette could not be seen.

It could, at times, get a little monotonous, but time was set aside for sailing and beach parties. We also had the odd stop at Famagusta to take on mail and stores.

"Stop and Search"

Leisure Time

End of the Commission

On our return to Malta from Cyprus, my eighteen month stint on the WooHa was up, and I was looking forward to going home.

The correspondence between myself and Vicki had got past the Just Friends stage and was now quite warm and loving. We had been regularly writing to each other and swapping photo's for the past eighteen months, and I was now extremely keen to find out just what was at the other end of all this correspondence.

Having said all my farewells to my mates on the WooHa, I travelled by truck to Luqa Airport and, bronzed and tanned, caught a plane bound for the UK and thirty six days home leave.

"Do you hear there. Laundry is now ready for connection, correction, collection.

*"Do You Hear there,
Bernard's Tailors, yesterday's fashions at tomorrows prices, is now on the dockside"*

HMS Woodbridge Haven 1956 - 1957　　　　　　　　　　　　Memories Are Made Of This

And Finally. . . . . .

Me and 'Deeps' (After)　　**Armier beach**　　**Lunch in the Communications Mess**

I'm not sure how to explain this photograph, except to say that she is definitely *not* my type!

It was Visitors Day in Messina, Sicily.

The Old Boy spoke about three words of English, and he had been gabbling and gesticulating to me for about half an hour, when I realised he wanted me to *marry* his Daughter!

We were on a Good Will visit, and I could see Sicily breaking off Diplomatic Relations.

Can't remember how I got out of this one but, with hindsight, I think I was lucky not to have found a horse head hidden in my hammock.

Stand Easy

Before I arrive home, let me digress for a moment and tell you a story. It might well be fiction, but this is how I heard it while in Malta, and I think it amply illustrates the Navy I had joined.

It concerns two characters, Lord Mountbatten who was, at that time, Commander in Chief of the Mediterranean, and an old Sailor called 'Stripey' Watson. Stripey had reached the rank of Able Seaman and stayed there. If Stripey got a chance to sign on for a few more years, he would do so just for the Rum Ration. He had been in a few actions during the war and now, with age and good conduct, had a fairly cushy life.

Now, if you wanted to make a complaint, you filled in a request form to see either your Divisional officer, the First Lieutenant or the Captain depending on how serious the complaint.

Apparently, Stripey had put in a request to see the Commander in Chief Mediterranean via the Flag officer via his Captain via etc etc. to make a complaint concerning a "personal and private matter". And, because it was a private matter, no one dared to ask what the problem was and, as his Request Form gradually worked its way up through the various chains of command, more and more people were getting curious trying to figure out what personal and private problem Stripey could possibly have to tell Mountbatten.

Eventually it gained him an audience with Mountbatten, his flag officer and several Staff officers at Mountbatten's residence. Both had served together during the war and greeted each other warmly and respectfully.

"Now, what can I do for you Watson?", asked Mountbatten.

"Well, it's rather private sir", replied Stripey nodding towards the entourage.

"Ah, I see", said Mountbatten dismissing his Staff except for the Flag Officer.

"Well, you see sir, it's my Daughter. She's joined the Wrens and they've sent her out here to Malta".

"Obviously to be near her Father, that's excellent, and what I would expect", replied Mountbatten.

"No, no, no sir, you don't understand. Each week she writes a letter home to the wife, and tells her everything I'm doing!".

"Ah!". said Mountbatten, "I see the problem. You leave this one with me Watson".

And a week later the daughter landed in Singapore.

Wasn't life wonderful before Feminism? Now it's time to catch that 'plane home. . . . .

Captions on a Postcard please.

Memories Are Made Of This

HMS Dundas

1957 - 1958

'But when the breezes blow, I generally go below'
W S Gilbert

Home Leave

While I had been in Malta, the family had moved from Paddington to 27 Worth Grove in Camberwell near Mum's sister Doris. The house in Walterton Road had been sold to a really nasty piece of work. He had got the teenage daughter of the family on the first floor pregnant, and she had an in-house back street abortion. I think he had also tried something similar with Mother, and she had ended up in hospital with a nervous breakdown, where she was being given, the then fashionable, electric shock treatment.

I caught a bus from Waterloo Station to Camberwell. I offered the Conductor my fare and asked him to let me know when we got to Camberwell Gate. Unexpectedly, he refused my fare and said something along the lines of what a wonderful job our boys had done at Suez, (which rather surprised me), and went on to say how much the country had been behind us, and how badly we had been let down by the Politicians. I felt something being lifted from my shoulders - it was that depressed feeling I had when we left Port Said.

The families new flat was small with two bedrooms, the second of which was minimal and already housed my two brothers Derek and Peter. However, the flat was also a short tube ride to Vicki's place in Smedley Street, Stockwell - and that is to where I had already plotted a course and was now headed.

Vicki's Dad was a School Keeper, and they had a nice detached schoolhouse in Smedley street next to a plot of Pre Fabs. I met Vicki in the kitchen and was introduced to her Mum a Dad. Vicki then made me a cup of coffee, which was the best I had ever tasted, and shortly after her Mum and Dad left us on our own.

There comes a time in every ones life when you make a decision that has an impact on the remainder of that life, and this was one of them.

We were standing some way apart, and you could cut the shyness with a knife - but I just had to go for it. I put down the coffee, took hold of her hand, pulled her in close to me and kissed her. From there on in it was all downhill.

Her Mum and Dad allowed me to stay at their place, sleeping on the living room floor in front of an open fire. After a couple of nights, Vicki would sneak downstairs and join me. We just use to sit in front of the fire facing each other, me in a sleeping bag and she wrapped in a blanket, talking for ages and occasionally throwing a bit more wood on the fire.

Apart from the odd kiss and cuddle, nothing happened. For me, this was different and, without the obligatory sink in the corner, I would not know where to begin. I was also trying to be a perfect gentleman and get the hang of this Romance thing that all the girls kept on about.

During the first week of my leave, I received the orders for my next draft which I had been hoping would have been based at Portsmouth, allowing me to see Vicki on a regular basis.

My new ship was to be HMS Dundas based at Portland and, when I checked the map and found that it was 140 miles from London, I realised that I would not be able to see her quite as often as I would have wished.

But we both enjoyed the rest of my leave and, although still nothing had happened, with all the late night chats I was beginning to see a little more into the future, and thought that the relationship was going somewhere.

HMS Dundas 1957 - 1958.   Memories Are Made Of This

Portland Bill and Weymouth

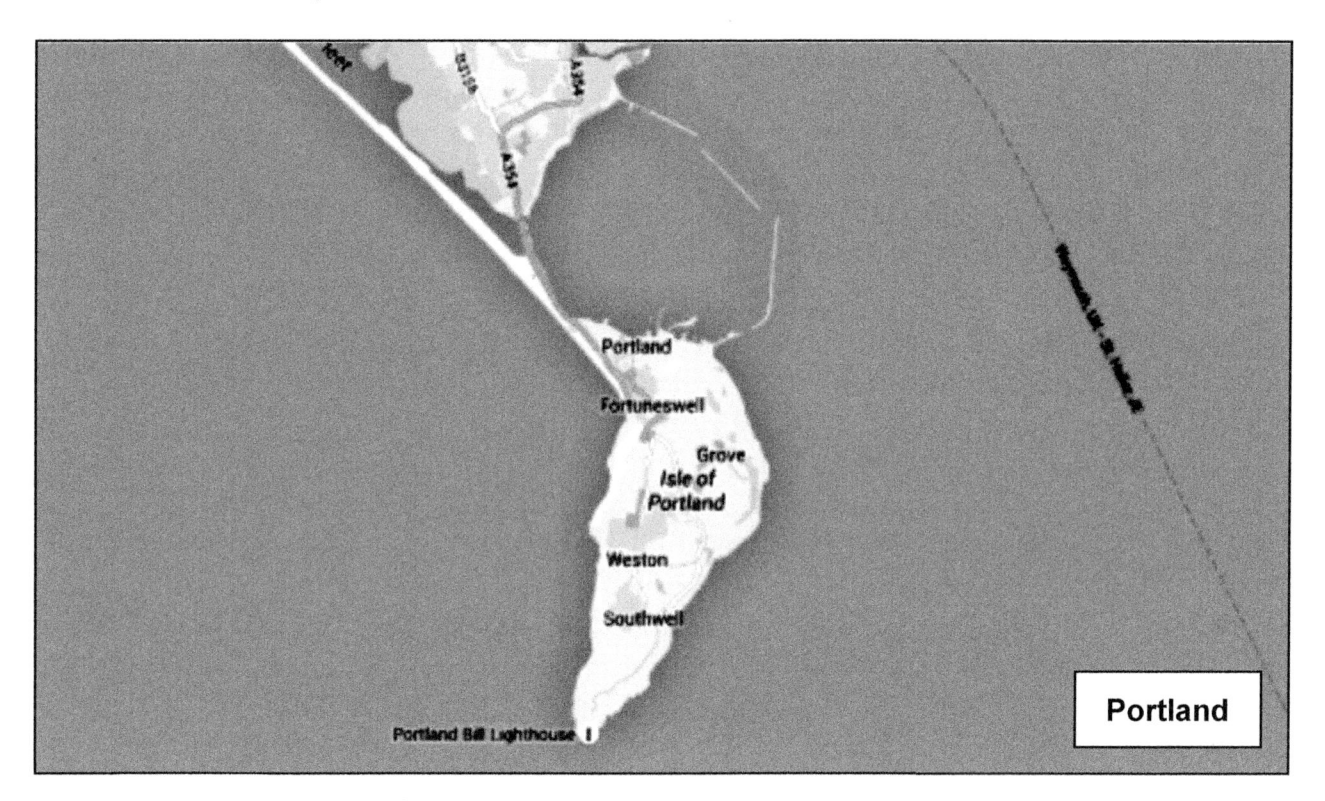

Looks OK on the map, but when you get there.....

"Do you hear there.
Will the ship's tennis team please return all rackets to the PTI, and balls to the Master at Arms".

Portland

Portland is a miserable, cold place at the best of times, and this was the end of November 1957 - and some years before the Government gave us Global Warming. I suppose I had got use to the Mediterranean sunshine and climate, and this made the place seem even more miserable.

HMS Dundas was a new type of frigate, designed for anti submarine warfare. She had one propeller which made manoeuvres in harbour difficult and, when at sea, she was thrown all over the place. The English Channel at Portland seemed to delight in giving her the roughest passage possible, and I cannot remember a time when I was not sea sick and praying for death.

So, having even today no desires to remain in Portland for too long, I will mention a couple of experiences and then move quickly on.

One day, while in harbour, I was called into the Coxswains office. He handed me a small package and said, "That's yours Lad. Sign 'ere". When I opened the package I found a Medal inside. I checked and it had my name and number on it, but I could not work out what it was for. I remembered, with some pride, that a few weeks earlier I had come second in the NAAFI queue, but I could not believe it was for that, so I asked the Coxswain.

He took the medal, looked at it and said, "It's a General Service medal Lad, were you at Suez?". Now I understood, and said thanks. "Don't thank me lad, thank Her Majesty, Gawd bless 'er". I thought Granddad Ash had medals, and that my Dad had WW2 medals - this was becoming a family tradition and, if one day I had a son.. I noticed that the clasp on the medal contained the words 'Near East' instead of 'Suez'. And I guess that the Politicians had made such a mess of the operation, that they no longer wished to be reminded of it.

During 1957, HMS Dundas was used to make the film 'Further up the creek', with Shirley Eaton and Frankie Howerd. Of the two, Frankie Howerd turned out to be the most popular with the ship's crew, but I was too young at the time to fathom the reason why.

We had a Good Will trip to Kiel in Germany, and travelled the length of the Kiel canal. I was struck by how few Germans waved to us and, from some, we even got the odd Hiel Hitler with the customary salute. I came away with distinct impression that the Germans were a little peeved about losing *both* wars - and they still had the 1966 World cup to live through.

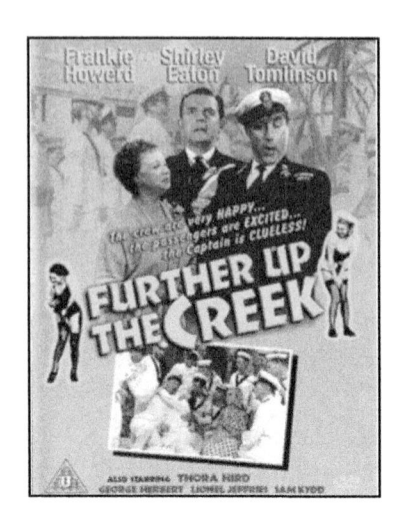

Demise of the ships crockery RIP (Rest in Pieces)

Weymouth

Portland's one and only redeeming compensation came about one afternoon as I was wandering along the seafront in Weymouth with Charlie, one of my mates on the Dundas.

It was a warm sunny afternoon, when I spotted an attractive blonde girl and her mate coming towards us. Now, the thing that had drew me to the blonde, was that she was the spitting image of Kathy Kirby, (a well known female singer at that time). And, having been handed one of the easiest Chat-Up lines, I said, 'Kathy Kirby, loved your last record'. And before she could reply, I took her hand and said, 'Let's have a drink and talk about it'. Then, turning to Charlie and the other girl, 'See you two later'.

Charlie did not look too pleased, but then I do not think that Charlie was too keen on the other one. Anyway, the blonde told me that her name was Faith and that she and her friend were having a Weekend in Weymouth. I then learned that Faith came from Damerham near Fordingbridge in Wiltshire, about ten miles south of Salisbury.

Apparently her father ran the local pub in Damerham called the Compasses Inn, a 400 year old Pub. This was getting interesting. We spent the rest of the afternoon and evening together, and completely forgot about meeting the other two. Faith invited me to stay with her at the pub the following weekend - so I did.

Weekend leave rotated over a three week period. First Weekend was from Friday evening until six Monday Morning. Second was from Saturday Lunch time, and the third you spent onboard as the Duty Watch. I spent every Weekend, (except one), with Vicki and we were slowly becoming lovers and I needed to see her more often.

About July 1958, the Navy was looking for volunteers to join the Submarine Service based at HMS Dolphin at Portsmouth. Now, Submariners received a higher rate of pay to their counter parts in the Navy, Portsmouth was much closer to Vicki with a good rail service and, most of all, this could be the cure for my sea sickness - I volunteered.

The Submariners course was quite intense and my only memory is the 100 feet deep Escape Tank. Beneath the tank is a water tight compartment and once inside, the compartment is flooded and you can swim underwater breathing through a tube connected to oxygen bottles. The hatch is then opened and you go though and just shoot to the surface 100 feet above - I loved it.

Unfortunately, I then got a nasty discharge from one of my ears, it would not go away and I knew I could not hide it from the medics. I failed, and my Submariners course came to an abrupt end, and I was drafted to HMS Yarnton, a Minesweeper based in Portsmouth. I was now based in Portsmouth and would be able to see Vicki more often. Was I in for a shock.

Compasses Inn, Damerham

Stand Easy

Time to take a quick break for another story, and this one is absolutely true, and can still be found today documented in the Admiralty archives.

During the war, a crusty old Admiral received a written report stating that the local Naval Stores were running short of uniforms, because the women, in the newly formed Wren Service, had been purchasing the navy blue serge to make their own uniforms.

The Admiral sent a signal addressed to the whole Navy, both Home and Abroad, in which the preamble outlined the problem, and his final paragraph read;

"Therefore, and in view of the above, all Wrens clothing is to be held up until the needs of the sea going man have been satisfied"

Wasn't life wonderful before Political Correctness? And it may be wishful thinking on my part, but I don't think that order was ever rescinded.

And, if you would like to know more about the Navy of that period, I would invite you to read a book called "Make a signal". The author, Jackie Broome, had access to the wartime Admiralty and Navy messages, and the book contains a collection of the most humorous.

Now it is time to join my third Minesweeper. . . . .

HMS Dundas in calmer waters

"Do you hear there. There will be an issue of tissue from the tissue issue room at 1500

Memories Are Made Of This

HMS Yarnton

1958 - 1959

'Give me a Boat and a Bucket'
Navy Anon

Cyprus Patrols

I knew every inch of a Minesweeper and did not need to be shown around, and I felt quite chipper as I arrived on board HMS Yarnton and stowed my gear. I was then approached by the Coxswain who casually informed me that if I wanted a long Weekend leave, I could go now but be back by six on Monday morning because we were sailing for Cyprus!

On the train up to Waterloo I struggled to find some way of telling Vicki as painlessly as possible, but we had a very sad, close and tearful Weekend.

I noticed that the four or five Officers we had on board looked very young an inexperienced and, because I had been on Cyprus Patrols before, I was invited to take part in a meeting with them, and I came away with the uneasy feeling that we would be groping our way in the dark. It was also going to be the first time in the Navy that I disobeyed an Order.

As we started to cross the Bay of Biscay, my old sea sickness problem took hold and I was violently sick all the way to Gibraltar but, although I did not know it at the time, this was the last time I would ever be sea sick, the Bay had cured me for good. En route we stopped at Gibraltar to replenish, and then again at Malta. Once in Malta for some strange reason I felt 'at home', and visited all the old haunts that Taff and I used to frequent. However, the WooHa and her clutch of Minesweepers that I had come to love were all gone. At Cyprus we took onboard a Cypriot Muslim interpreter and, for reasons that I couldn't fathom at the time, the Chef insisted that we all had Bacon Butties for breakfast.

At Cyprus we had a monotonous routine of anchoring during the day, and patrolling from dusk until dawn, and I cannot remember ever stopping a ship. (When we patrolled on the WooHa we stopped and boarded at least one Merchantman per day and, at night we would sail along close into the shoreline with the ship darkened and everyone watching the Radar and listening on the radios).

After a week or so we would return to the small Naval Base at Famagusta. By the quay where we tied up, and quite close to the ship, there was a small working party of Naval engineers working in the open on various bits of machinery. During the day, one of he ships crew took a four hour turn to guard the gangway armed with a Lanchester rifle slung over the shoulder. One afternoon it was my turn and, after a couple of hours I noticed this old Cypriot man coming through the gate. I removed the Lanchester from my shoulder, and asked him where he was going but he could not speak English. Just then the Chief of the working party called across to me that he was OK ,and that he ran errands for them. At that moment one the ships officers appeared at the gangway and shouted at me, "Shoot him Ash! Shoot him!". I slung the Lanchester back over my shoulder as the Chief, with a look of total disbelief, informed the officer in no uncertain terms that the man was "One of ours".

However, I had a feeling that once back on board I was going to be in trouble. I had not so much as disobeyed an order as totally ignored it. And, before finishing for the day, the Chief tapped me on the shoulder and said that if there was a problem onboard I could rely on him to speak for me. - in the Navy there was always a helping hand somewhere.

Anyway, when I got back on board, not a word was said. And this was probably helped by the fact that the officer did not speak to me for about three days - Dipstick!

Round about the end of November 1958 I was suddenly told that I was being sent home for a months leave, (Great!), prior to being drafted to HMS Cavalier in the Far East for an eighteen month stint.

Forelocks, rowlocks, haddocks and bollards! How was I going to explain *that* to Vicki?

Stand Easy

Time for another story. I cannot remember where I heard this one, I may even have read it in the book that I mentioned earlier called Send a Signal, but it goes something like this.

An Admiral on board a Cruiser was putting a squadron of four Destroyers through their paces by ordering various exercises and manoeuvres whilst under steam. Onboard one of the Destroyers, under the command of the most junior commander of the four Destroyers, was a group of civilian photographers and gentlemen from the Press, who had been invited to watch and report on the proceedings. The exercises and manoeuvres had been going well, and the Commander was determined to impress his passengers with his nautical skills.

The Admiral then ordered each Destroyer in turn to take up a parallel position alongside the Cruiser, at a distance of forty yards, maintain the position for a mile and then peel off and take up their station astern of the cruiser. All went well with the first three ships, then came the turn of the fourth who, unfortunately, misjudged the turning circle and managed to scrape the side of the cruiser and, before he had time to get back on station at the rear, the Cruiser's Aldis lamp started to wink.

"Message from the Admiral, sir" said the Signal man to the Commander handing him the message in front of the Press.

"Read it out", said the Commander.

The Signalman, looking a little sheepish, said, "From the Admiral, to us. Message reads, You blithering, blundering idiot. If you ever try another manoeuvre like that again I will have you Courts Martialled. Message ends sir"

"Very good" said the Commander. "Take it below to the Wireless Office, and have it decoded".

Now, where had I got to? Oh yes, Vicki. . . . .

"Do you hear there, Would the person who dropped a five pound note in the dinning hall, please fall in three deep outside the regulating office."

Memories Are Made Of This

HMS Cavalier

1959 - 1960

'The merry Mariners are bold and free'
P B Shelly

The Far East

I had a great welcome home from Vicki and the first week was great, but I could see her face drop and the disappointment when I told her what was coming next. However, I had already spoken to her Mum and Dad and, having gained their permission, I asked her to marry me. She accepted, and we became engaged, and we planned to get married as soon as I was home from the Far East. Of all the farewells that we had lived through, this was the saddest.

And although I knew that the next eighteen months in the Far East could be the best I had yet experienced, I still left with a heavy heart. I cannot remember where we flew from, possibly Heathrow, but it took four days to reach Singapore, with a one day stop in Bangkok.

HMS Cavalier was an old but beautiful wartime Destroyer. With three four point five gun turrets, Anti Aircraft guns, Torpedo tubes and a fast rate of knots. Even tied up at the quay she looked every bit the fighting greyhound of the sea that she was. What a ship, what a privilege.

As with any new crew, the first two weeks are spent at sea for a Work Up period where you put the ship through her paces and get to know every nut, bolt and rivet in your department, and it was during this busy period that I received my first letter from Vicki - and it was not good news.

Vicki had written that she had missed her last period, and had asked her Mum if she thought it was because I was away. Her Mum had replied that would depend on what he had been doing while he was at home which, by now, was not much of a secret. I was a very worried man.

I was half way around the world and, because the crew had not yet had a chance to get to know one another, I had no one to turn to to discuss matters of a compassionate nature - the only time in the Navy that I could not see a helping hand. However, the next postbag about two weeks later brought good news. Vicki was now ticking over as regular as clockwork so, with a sigh of relief, I settled down to a commission that would turn out to be my best eighteen months in the Navy with the best ship, best Captain and best Crew.

The whole of our eighteen months commission is well documented in a book that we had printed at the time, so I am only going to relate my own personal experiences which would not normally be 'Mentioned in Dispatches'.

Cavaliers Radio Operators Singapore

Hong Kong - Getting Acclimatised

Once we had settled down and paid our first visit to Hong Kong, (Hong Kong? That's where the Men are Men, and the Women continuously remind them of it), and having listened to the stories about the Far East from the more experienced Hands, and paid a visit to Pinkies the local Tattooing artist, I was beginning to like the place.

All the Bars in Hong Kong had girls in them and, for the girls, it was a great honour if they had regular boy friends. And because we were paid fortnightly, we had this wonderful working arrangement where you would look after the girl for a week then she would look after you for the next week.

Hong Kong was also saturated with American sailors who had far more money than us, so we would go to the China Fleet Club and have cheap drinks until about fifteen minutes to midnight.

At midnight, all American Sailors had to be back on their ships regardless of rank and, as they were coming out, we were going in with the girls rushing up to greet us - the Americans hated it, even though we always wished them a cheery polite 'Good Night chaps'.

But, even though the girls were very accommodating, with warm balmy nights of love and no face slapping, it did have its down side.

They were quite keen to have a Eurasian child and, if you failed in your duty that month, you got a week's worth of, "You! No bloody good in bed!", and, "You! Bloody Cherry boy". (Cherry boy? A Virgin, or possibly worse). Then, about week later, you would be completely forgiven.

It took a bit of getting use to.

We had a Chinese Tailor onboard Cavalier and he was responsible for all the suits and silk waist coats.

Pinkies

Hong Kong Boxing Day 1959 Sing Bar

Life in Harbour

One evening, in a Hong Kong Bar, we met a young American sailor who seemed to have rather a lot to say about the quote British Navy's Rum Ration Unquote.

So, always looking for an opportunity to improve the UK/USA 'Special Relationship', he was cordially invited by a number of us to come round the following day at noon, and sample our hospitality and Rum - which he duly did.

The rest of Cavalier's Crew had, of course, also been informed of the arrival of our American guest and, after having had numerous Wets and Sippers of Rum from members of the Communications mess, he was then a little surprised to find the rest of the Crew insisting that he had a wet of theirs.

He then fell asleep and, although courtesy and hospitality dictated that he should not be disturbed, we were, nevertheless, a little surprised to find him still fast asleep the following morning.

Cavalier entering Harbour

"Do you hear there. Able Seaman Bird, lay aft"

North Malaya - Bandit Country

Some time into the commission, Cavalier was taken into the dry dock in Singapore for a six week refit. We were lodged in the local shore establishment HMS Terror and, with its own swimming pool and sport facilities, there was plenty to keep us entertained. There was also an opportunity for four of us to spend two weeks with the Army, who were fighting the Communist Bandits, in the north of Malaya. Four of us volunteered, and spent a day and a half in a sleeper train getting there.

We were met and greeted by a giant of an Australian soldier who took us back to the Army camp in the jungle. At the Camp we were first issued with a shortened 303 rifle, two belts of ammunition and clothing, and then taken to the Cookhouse for a meal. After that, he took us to a beer tent and introduced us to the Army chaps. We soon discovered that it was a mixture of British and Australian troops. There was also a New Zealand troop who were at that time in the jungle, had been ambushed and taken some casualties. Last, but not least, there was a company of Gurkhas who literally lived in the jungle.

The Army showed us everything, and I was amazed how they were clearing out the Bandits. They had a big map of Malaya divided into squares. The white squares showed the cleared areas, and the black where the Bandits were known to be. From the map you could see the black squares being pushed back to the Border. Compare that with the Americans in Vietnam.

One day we were taken to quite a famous hill where the Army was building a Road and, to get there we had to go through a couple of black squares, but we felt safe in a Land rover and armed to the teeth. However, on the way back the Land rover broke down, and we had no radio communications. Four hours or so later a big armoured wheeled vehicle, that had been sent to find us, arrived and towed us back to base. We had broken down in a square with a black patch.

In the Beer tent one night, we were told that the Gurkhas didn't believe that a Bandit was dead, until the Bandit had been cut up into small pieces about the size of an Oxo cube and, for the Army, this made identification of the deceased decidedly difficult, and somewhat messy. So an Army Intelligence Officer approached the Gurkhas, and told them that their great white Queen, in the big house in London, would like the heads of her enemies for the mantelpiece. To which the Gurkhas respectfully concurred and duly obliged and, from then on, identification became a doddle. Now, the story may well have been the beer talking and, consequently, subject to a *slight* degree of exaggeration - but I still believe it.

The photographs overleaf, taken by an Army Specialist, speak for themselves, and I do not want to dwell on it, except to say that, since then, I have had a great admiration and respect for the Army - there is no way I could have lived or done a job like that, and their Malaya medal was well deserved.

"Do us a favour, call the AA"

HMS Cavalier 1959 - 1960   Memories Are Made Of This

North Malaya - Bandit Country

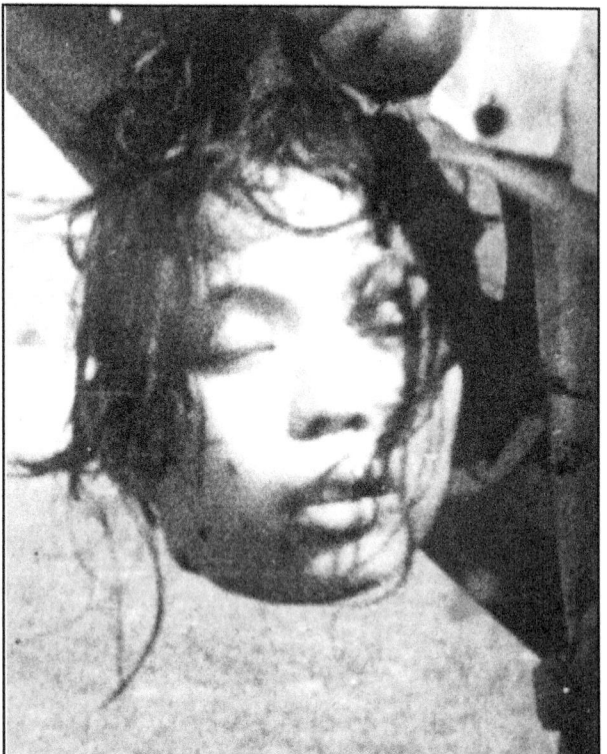

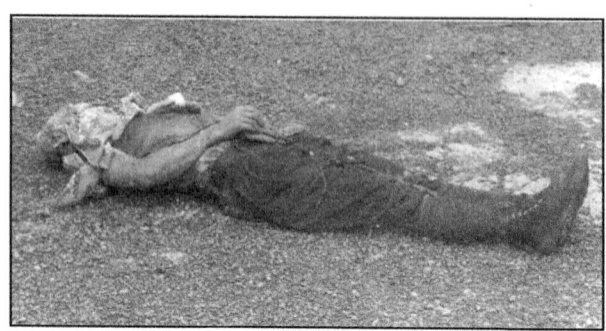

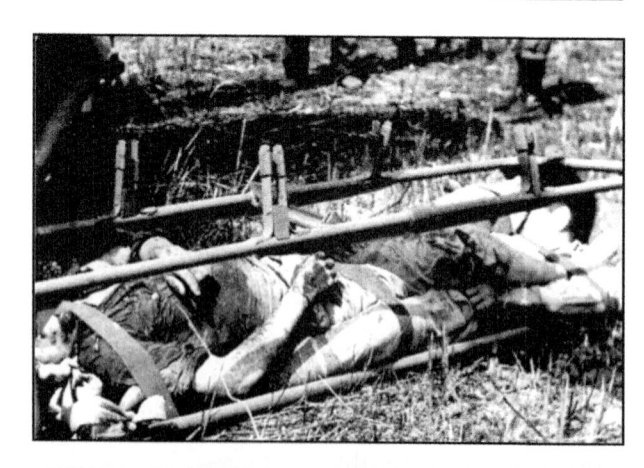

64

The Antipodes

Before we arrived in Australia, we had spent some thirteen months sailing between Tokyo, Saigon, Singapore, Malaya, Manila, and Hong Kong, and we had all got acclimatised to the Chinese Ladies. Now, I am not saying that all Chinese girls are extremely flat chested, but it was generally agreed that, if you were in trouble, you could safely land a light aircraft on one.

So, when we docked at our first Australian port, Freemantle, you can imagine our amazement, after thirteen months, to discover the dock lined with dozens of dazzling females, with whom you had *no* chance of landing a 'plane - none whatsoever. I think the whole Crew, including myself, were suffering in various degrees from a combination of BWS and BDS, (Boob Withdrawal Symptoms and Boob Deficiency Syndrome). But, (to coin a phrase), relief was at hand.

When we arrived at Adelaide, we found the Australian female hospitality was the same as it had been in Freemantle. I was casually strolling through the town one late afternoon, when a gorgeous girl ran up to me, grabbed my arm and said, "Help me, there's a Dago, (which I thought was an Australian Dog), following me". I offered to walk her home.

We walked for about forty minutes and seemed to be getting farther away from the town. We ended up on a bench in a beautiful Park just after dusk, and we made love on the bench.

As we were both, to coin another phrase, adjusting our dress, I noticed this Policeman walking towards us and, as he got close and saw my uniform his attitude changed a little, and he politely asked if we were both OK. I asked if everything was alright, and he replied "Fine Cobber, enjoy your stay" - I already had.

I still think to this day that he was probably watching us all the time. Anyway I walked her back to town where we parted company, and it was not until I got back on board that I realized that we had not even exchanged names. Is it any wonder then that, later in life, I often received complaints from my female partner about my lack of romance.

On our way around to Sydney, the talk in the Mess was all about the fabulous Adelaide females, so you can imagine our joy as we approached the dock in Sydney to find it lined with most of the girls from Adelaide - they knew when we were due to dock in Sydney and had travelled en masse. I was beginning to love this country with its tasteful tactile traditions.

While in Sydney we apparently caused a little bit of embarrassment to the British Embassy. We had so many invitations to stay at peoples homes that, even after sending the men under punishment and the Duty Watch ashore, the invitations were still rolling in, and the Embassy was getting some very irate phone calls. But by now the ship was empty. Anyone could have walked along the dock, gone on board and, if they knew how to start it, sailed away.

I stayed with a young married couple. They took us everywhere, including a Drive In Movie which I had never seen before, and gave us a great time as well as steak for breakfast.

The thing I liked most about the Australians was that they were all down to earth with no airs and graces. It was a great trip, a great country, with the most hospitable people I had yet come across.

However, although I have never been back, I have to say at this juncture that, if today's Australia is anything like the way it is portrayed in the TV program "Neighbours" then, dear friends, you really have gone down hill fast and *completely* lost the plot .

Singapore

During the Commission, Singapore gained it's independence and, in the weeks prior to the handover, there was a hive of activity from would be Singapore Politicians and political parties.

Not least amongst these was the Peoples Action Party, (PAP), who would tell the electorate that if they liked the PAP, to put a great big cross alongside their name on the Ballot Form and, if they didn't like the PAP, just put a small cross.

Guess who won the election?

Cavalier entering Singapore

"Do you hear there. The NAAFI is now open and will remain open until.......... it closes"

HMS Cavalier 1959 - 1960   Memories Are Made Of This

Far East Leisure Time

Motor Fishing Vessel Expedition, South China Seas

Mallaca Beach

MFV Trip. Training a new Sparks

China Fleet Club just before midnight

The Maldive Islands

Whilst we with several other ships were visiting Cochin in west India, we were suddenly ordered to put to sea for an unknown destination.

We left the other ships in harbour, travelling in a south westerly direction at a speed which caused the ships stern to vibrate alarmingly.

The Radio Operators, (who always knew everything before anyone else), were bombarded with questions from the rest of the crew all wanting to know what was up. We didn't know, and I guess the Orders must have been delivered on board by hand.

However, when we were well out to sea the Captain gave us a briefing over the Tannoy system. We were heading for the Maldive Islands. Apparently, on one of the islands, Gan, the British company Costains were building a Runway for the RAF, and both thought that they were under threat from the Islands inhabitants.

Our Orders were to get there ASAP and protect the 'British Interests'.

As one of the British Interests happened to be the local Bar selling the cheapest booze in the Far East, 'ASAP' and 'protection' took on a whole new meaning. (When I went into the Bar and ordered a Drambuie, it was served in a pint glass. Either the Barman was new to the game or extremely pleased to see us).

As we approached the Maldives, it looked as though there were palm trees growing out of the sea. This is because the highest point of land is only about a meter or so above sea level, and does not become visible until you are almost on top of it - a sight to be seen.

Addu Atoll is horseshoe shaped. The opening is narrow, quite shallow and, in the clear water, you could see a dozen or so sharks patrolling the entrance.

We anchored in the middle of the atoll where the water was quite deep with good fishing.

And here we stayed, with the odd patrol, until we were relieved by a sister ship a month later.

Arrival at Gan, Addu Atoll

You are to assist the RAF to defend . . . . .

The Maldive Islands

During the month, everything onboard was relaxed with numerous beach parties, Bar-B-Qs, fishing competitions, evening film shows and fashion parades. The latter consisted of dressing anyway that took your fancy or, to quote the Daily Orders at that time, "Dress of the Day; Three Ply Lanyards and Brown Smoke Puffs". We seemed to blend in quite well, and it soon became difficult to tell the difference between us and the Natives.

Situated close to the Equator, we invited the RAF to spend a day at sea with us to observe the traditional Crossing the Line ceremony, and we had a great day at sea. However, Gan did have one solitary downside for which we all blamed the Captain. He had steamed at such a speed that, due to the vibration, every tin of milk had solidified and turned into an inedible form of cheese that was impossible to pour but, after we had discovered the Bar prices and the laid back living, he was positively forgiven.

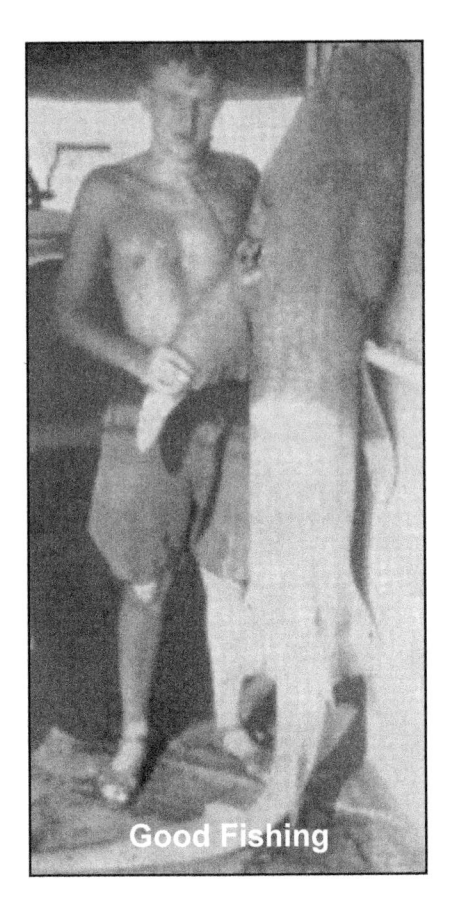

Good Fishing

The Sun Deck

Missionary Position

King of the Catwalk

At Anchor in the middle of the lagoon

The RAF on Gan

The RAF on Gan made us feel very welcome but, as is quite normal in these circumstances, there were the odd episodes of mild inter Services rivalry, as the following story indicates.

The following extract is quoted from the RAF Gan Web site. Author: Ian (Jock) Morrison BRFP

Quote: Britain responded to this threat by sending the famous Royal Navy Destroyer HMS Cavalier, two armed Shackletons and a Dakota to Addu. The arrival of the Cheshires, RAF Regiment and the Royal Navy, surprisingly enough, caused no friction whatsoever. We all got on very well. The NAAFI, already stretched regarding accommodation, was often bursting at the seams. On occasion, sailors would miss their Liberty boat and spend the night in the kadjans. They could sleep anywhere, those lads. One spent the night on our table, legs hanging off one end, head lolling back off the other. Others slumped in chairs, others on the floor.

Once, in the middle of the night, the navy came ashore and painted in large letters on the white runway,

"RAF GAN, UNDER THE CARE AND PROTECTION OF H M ROYAL NAVY".

The insult must have been visible from the moon! My colleagues decided to retaliate by borrowing canoes and sneaking out in the dark to paint funny faces along the side of the ship. I tried to talk them out of it, as I felt sure the navy would be prepared. But they insisted. I stayed on shore. They rowed out to the ship, armed with cans of paint and brushes, but, just as they were closing in, the ships floodlights came on, searchlights combed the water, and my colleagues were treated to buckets of gash and well-aimed fire hoses. They returned to Gan soaked and defeated. I didn't dare say, 'I told you so'.

On another occasion, sailors came to the kadjans with an open invitation to go aboard HMS Cavalier and witness the 'Crossing the Line ceremony'. Everybody declined except one, who went like a lamb to the slaughter. As everybody else had suspected, he wasn't invited aboard the ship to observe the ceremony, but to be the prime victim of it. Unquote

Ah, bless, I remember him well - nice lad, and I was about the twentieth in line to reluctantly follow him. However, in defence of my Cavalier colleagues I have to say that, although our endeavours were *always* undertaken in accordance with the tradition and spirit of Nelson's navy, our strict adherence to the "Rules of Engagement" may have been a trifle lax.

Gan Album

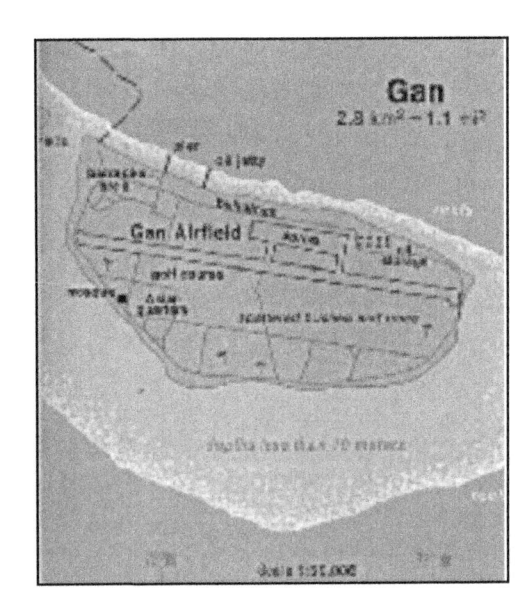

HMS Cavalier 1959 - 1960   Memories Are Made Of This

Mike Foster - The Chippies Mate

Mike Foster served on board Cavalier at the same time as myself, and kindly emailed me some of his memories of the time, and I thought that they were well worth recording.

Author: Mike Foster -Torpedo and Anti Submarine Branch (UC3).

I was on the '59/60 commission. Cavalier was my second ship, and I was just a little bit in awe of her reputation before I joined. As a TAS rate (UC3), prior to flying out to her I did a PCT in Vernon. That's where I learned that she was already the best ship in the Far East Fleet and with a top speed in excess of 35 knots, the fastest ship in the Royal Navy, (though I'm led to believe Manxman was pretty close at that time). I'm glad to say that our commission did not let her down in any way. I seem to remember she was named 'Cock of the Fleet' for winning most if not all the trophies for sporting and efficiency tests.

I have read your memoirs of the time and like you, it was my best and most memorable draft. Although you didn't say, it was some way into SEATO Exercise Jet 59 when as duty guard ship we slipped and proceeded from Cochin to Gan at high speed. As a seaman I was particularly pissed off at the time, because, as I remember it, we had just secured from mooring to head and stern buoys in the midst of a monsoon, when the Tannoy announced that we were under orders to slip and proceed. The Captain outlined our mission as soon as we cleared the shoreline, which was to proceed at all haste to Gan and provide naval support to the beleaguered RAF Station. On the way we broke out and primed ammunition for all of the guns, and for the final approach, illuminated the fighting lights and flew the battle ensign. Only to be met by a small group of fishing boats. The story emerged that a cell of communist agitators had stirred up the locals who were blowing up concrete as fast as Costain's could lay it.

Apparently, some of the locals were upset that those of them that had work on Gan could obtain luxuries, like soap, etc, from the NAAFI there, and they all wanted a share. They were a bit upset about restricted access to their fishing areas too. You may remember that we did our bit by blasting a large hole in the reef with a couple of our squid bombs, thus allowing access via a different route. I believe the rest of it was eventually resolved by allowing all the locals to shop in the NAAFI. It was good fun there though. I enjoyed flying patrols in their Dakota, the swimming and pissing off the RAF by helping to demolish their corporals mess (all four banana leaves of it)! We went there twice.

It was also during Ex Jet 59 that HMS Hogue collided with INS Mysore. What a sorry mess she was, but Mysore was hardly scratched! Do you remember having to leave Hong Kong to escort a British vessel through the Straights of Formosa (as it was then called)? She had been hit by shells exchanged between the Chinese Communist and Nationalist armies off Quemoy.

I also enjoyed Saigon, Japan, Manila and Australia (who wouldn't?). I also enjoyed my six weeks foreign service leave. I arrived home with five hand made sharkskin shirts, three made to measure suits, a Gabardine raincoat and hand made shoes, as well as a tiddly new uniform. Never been so well dressed, before or since.

I was a native of Margate at that time and during that leave I just happened to bump into Arty Shaw who was down the visiting his mum in hospital. Needless to say, my mum took him in for a couple of days and we had a few good runs. I met Joe Loveday briefly in Pembroke (RNBC) and again when he joined HMS Keppel in Portland - a place I seemed doomed to be at throughout. Osprey, Undaunted, Keppel, Russel and others in between.

Mike Foster. (ex Chippies Mate).

Crossing The Line Certificate

In Singapore there was reputed to be an old Chinese Herbalist, who sold pills that guaranteed pregnant women that the baby would be a boy, providing that they took the pills in the early stages of the pregnancy.

He also promised to refund the cost of the pills if they failed to work. And, true to his word, he did just that.

Result, everyone a winner and, even with all the refunds, he made a pile of money.

HMS Cavalier 1959 - 1960   Memories Are Made Of This

Cavalier's Stokers

A fine body of men, worthy in all respects to adorn these pages. And to whom the Captain, (allegedly), once said;

"Get below you rats, and give me steam!"

Tony Simms, Don Whalen, Bill Akrigg and LME Lazero.

Reg Bartlet and Fez Parker

Jock Forbes

Barry Elton

Barry Elton and Ted

Unknown and LME Lazero.

Charlie Bicknell

Ted Beaney, Bill Akrigg and Don Whalen

Life at sea

Cavalier under steam

Firing a torpedo was usually followed by a Tannoy message along the lines of, "Did anyone see where that one went?".

I think our torpedoes were the only ones in the Navy with our name and address painted on them, but I cannot recall ever recovering one.

Probably why the Tubes were later removed.

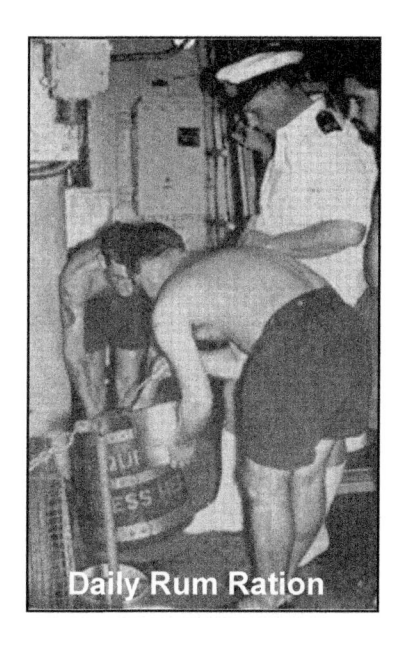

Daily Rum Ration

Torpedo Practice

Life at sea

Whilst travelling between Hong Kong and Singapore, Cavalier ran into a Typhoon that ripped a large lengthwise gash in the side of the ship just above the waterline. We returned to Hong Kong with the ship heavily listing away from the breached side and, for the return trip, we had to wee uphill.

Cavalier in a Hong Kong Dry Dock undergoing repairs.

HMS Cavalier 1959 - 1960   Memories Are Made Of This

Keith Crawford - Gun Layer 'B' Turret

Keith served on board Cavalier at the same time as myself, and kindly emailed me some of his memories of the time, and I thought that they were well worth recording.

Author: Keith Crawford -Torpedo and Anti Submarine Branch (UW).

January 1959 Junior seamen Keith Crawford landed Singapore to join HMS Cavalier.

Off to sea on my first ship, and I wondered how I would get on. For action stations, I will be a layer on B Gun - I didn't know a thing about guns, but soon to learn under the command of Sub Lt Tricky and Gunners Mate Bert Brooks, who had been on the Prince of Wales. He said, 'Boy, you will fire the gun if we go into local command'.

All the Juniors were looking forward to Hong Kong and once there, three of us were off to the bars in Wanchai There we found the Skyroom Ballroom where, for 10 Hk dollars to the Mamasan and the same to the girls, we had our Cherries plucked. After the event, looking at her dressing table with all the photos of the men she had known, one thought what next could one catch.

Off to sea to practiced Action Stations. Fired B Gun but no bang . Had to wait half an hour to unload, I then inspected the cartridge for a strike hit, and then threw it over board.

Next Port of call Saigon nice place still had French feel about it. Hong Kong for Christmas, and was invited up to the heights for Christmas eve, with best bib and tucker on little finger extended. Had a good time. Then to Singapore on exercise where we caught the tail end of a Typhoon that split the port side hull and fuel tanks. Returned to Hong Kong for Dry Dock repairs. No room at HMS Tamar, so we were billeted in the China Fleet Club - that's better. But we had to de-ammunition the ship first. Off to Tokyo got there all the others had left So off into Tokyo found the New Tokyo bar. Learned how to answer phone mushy mushy and a few more things with the hostess.

Off to Australia, and got 8 or 9 days leave in Adelaide, and rejoined the ship in Sydney - just in time for a night out in Kings Cross with some of the lads and girls. Defaulters next day will learn one day. Finished punishment just in time for a run ashore in Darwin.

Off to Cochin but fate takes a hand , and off we go to Gan in the Maldive Islands. Costain's Bar, threepence a nip! Fishing Competition on board, I caught a Shark and won everything. Lt Tricky fired 3 or 4 shots at it but I never found any bullet holes in it. So much for a Gunnery Officer.

June 1960 was here, and now for a 26 hour flight home. Had a smashing time with all. Feel sorry that lots of 16 17 year olds will never have the fun and laughs and comradeship that I enjoyed on the Cavalier. I can remember faces but names seem to have gone it was 52 years ago so THANKS TO ALL.
Keith Crawford

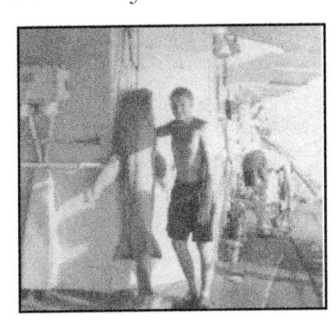

The Flag Officer's Inspection

The Flag Officer's inspection took place over a two day period. The first day we had the Sea inspection followed, on the second day, by the Harbour inspection.

The former consisted of putting Cavalier through her paces, testing the guns and torpedoes, and our procedures for Action Stations, fire fighting and a nuclear attack.

The Harbour inspection consisted of the Flag Officer giving various orders to the 1st Lieutenant, who would then Tannoy them through the ship. In the meantime, the Flag Officer's second in command would make notes on the response times - and we did not get off to a good start.

At about two in the afternoon, the Flag Officer's car arrived and parked some fifty yards from the ships gangway. The 1st Lieutenant, whose job it was to greet the Flag Officer, left the ship, approached the car and opened the door but, before he could salute, the Flag Officer ordered, "Drop the port anchor". The 1st Lieutenant came racing back to the ship shouting, "Drop the port anchor. Drop the port anchor".

Once the Flag Officer was ensconced on the Bridge, the orders over the Tannoy came thick and fast. Two of which still stick in my memory.

The first came about halfway through the afternoon when the order, "All men with tattoos to the port side of the ship" was quickly followed, as Cavalier began to keel over, by "Belay the last order. As you were!".

The second came towards the end of the inspection with the order, "Launch a Sputnik", and I remember saying to myself at the time, I think the old boy has probably snookered us with that one.

However, as I was afterwards informed, two minutes later the Petty Officer Chef arrived on the Bridge with a twelve inch wooden ruler in one hand and, in the other, a large potato with four matchsticks jutting out of the sides. In view of everyone, he went to the edge of the Bridge and, using the ruler, casually flicked the potato over the side of the ship. He then turned to the 1st Lieutenant, saluted and said, "Spudnik launched, but failed to go into orbit sir".

Up until that moment, none of us had ever realised or appreciated that, lodged amongst the pots and pans of Cavalier's galley, we had a NASA scientist in our midst.

DTG	110658 / APRIL	ROUTINE
FROM:	F.O.2.F.E.S.	UNCLASSIFIED
TO:	CAVALIER	

1. THANK YOU VERY MUCH FOR A VISIT WHICH I GREATLY ENJOYED.

2. IT WAS GOOD TO SEE CAVALIER IN SUCH GOOD SHAPE AND IN SUCH GOOD HEALTH.

Far East Commission

During the Commission, Cavalier was exercising with a squadron of United States navy ships consisting of five Destroyers headed by a Cruiser. The ships were in a line astern of each other, with the Cruiser in the lead and Cavalier at the rear. The Cruiser released a Drone, (a small radio controlled aircraft), for the ships to practice their gunnery. As the Drone flew down the line, each ship would fire in turn. The Americans seem to open up with everything they had but, although their firepower was awesome to watch, the Drone continued on it's way down the line towards Cavalier.

Now I ought to explain that Cavalier's guns were controlled by a Radar system but, at some time during their life, both the Radar system and guns had decided to break off their relationship, and they rarely spoke to each other.

However, our gun crews had what today would be called a 'Cunning Plan' - High Explosive Shells. With one of these you could miss by a decent distance and still deliver a fair degree of damage. As all three guns simultaneously fired a single broadside, there was a deafening bang followed by a cloud of acrid smoke and, as the smoke cleared, all you could see were hundreds of bits and pieces of the Drone slowly fluttering in the breeze, and drifting lazily towards the sea.

The Americans, who were even more surprised than we were, were so impressed that they positioned us to lead the fleet back into harbour.

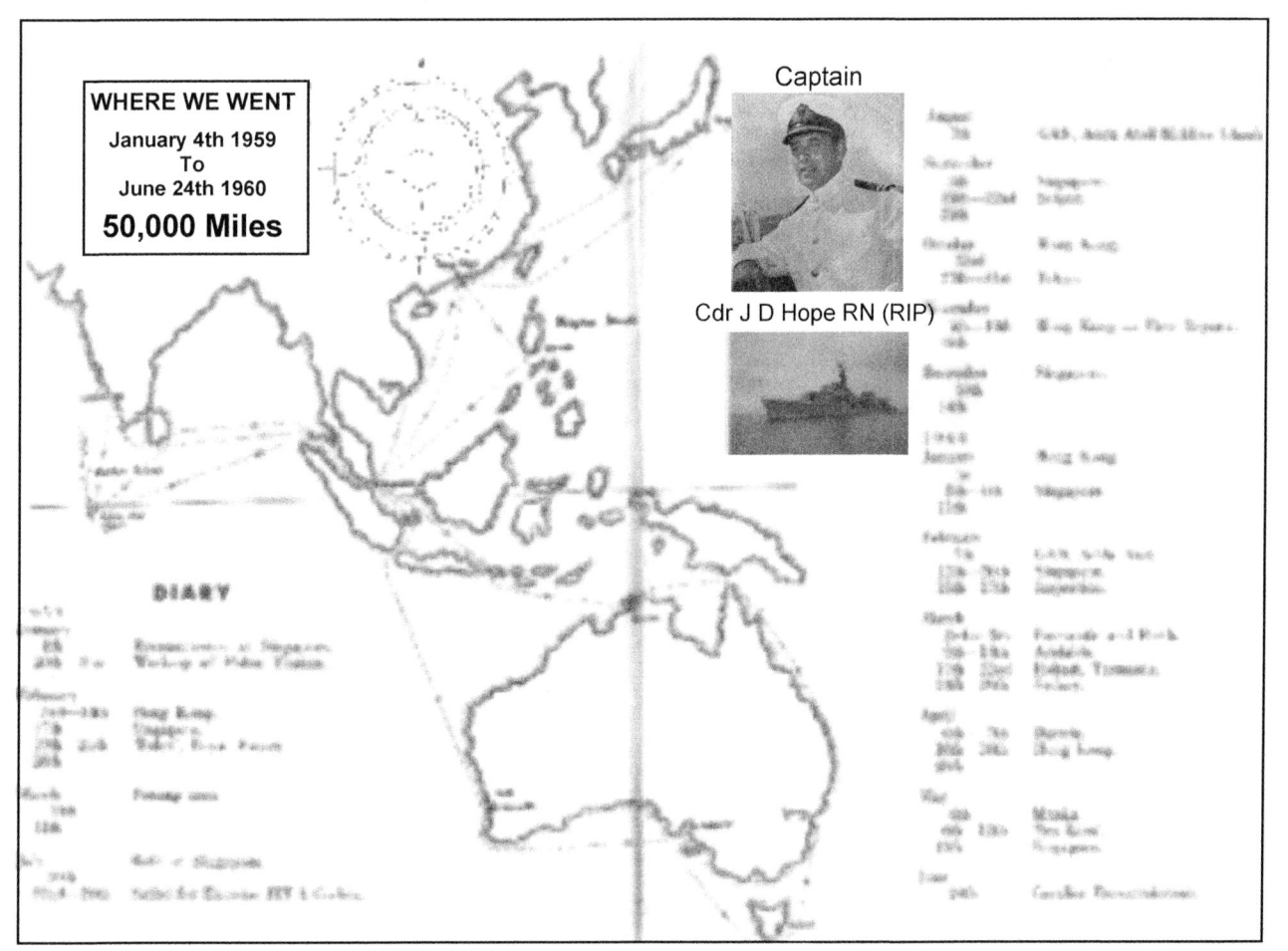

HMS Cavalier 1959 - 1960　　　　　　　　　　　　　　　　　　　　　Memories Are Made Of This

Life Ashore

China Fleet Club...

Cabaret Act.

We had a wonderful Christmas meal in the China Fleet Club in Hong Kong. This was followed by a Chinese Cabaret Act.

Whilst Cavalier was undergoing a refit in Singapore, we were lodged in the shore base HMS Terror.

It had excellent sports facilities, and a big open air swimming pool.

The last photograph of Cavaliers 1959/1960 Bunting Tossers and Sparkers together.

Back row, L to R;
Arty (RIP), Me, Stan, Poynton, J.R., Mick, Chas.

Front Row, L to R;
Joe, Tug, Charles.

Of all the Gin Joints in all the world. . . .

Finally, and no matter how much I would *love* to, I cannot leave Hong Kong and the Far East without mentioning, (long pause), Lilly. I am probably going to be called naive for this experience and, at odd times when I have related it before, I have always been told that I was seduced. If that *is* the case, then I am *not* complaining.

It was two in the afternoon on a warm, sunny day in Hong Kong, and I and two of my mates were *genuinely* out shopping for presents to take home with us. We came across a deserted Bar, and we decided to sit down at one of the tables and have a San Miguel, the local beer. I had not been sat down for more than ten minutes when I felt these soft, cool feminine hands massaging the back of my neck. My head dropped to one side, my eyes went glassy and my beer became a blur. When I turned round and my eyes became focused, there was a slim Chinese women wearing a silk Cheongsam, probably in her late twenties or early thirties, not bad looking with, can you believe, *boobs*.

Now, when you have not seen one of these for some time, to be suddenly confronted by *two* is totally out of order. It turned out that she wanted to take me back to her flat and there was no money involved. This was different. We got a Cab back to her place and in the Cab I asked why she had picked me, she replied that she was feeling very sexy and wanted me. I kept telling myself that there had to be a catch somewhere - but there wasn't. She was genuine.

Her flat was small, clean and comfortable. I sat down in an arm chair, while she put on some music. and started slowly dancing in front of me as she undressed. I reached out for her but she pushed me away saying, "No, no. First I undress you, and give you a bath". When I was in the bath, she gave me a drink and got in with me - this was nothing like the obligatory corner sink with which I had become accustomed and, minus both clothes *and* boots, I felt that I had definitely moved up in the world.

And, by the time we had got on the bed I was quite keen to get started but, every time I tried she would stop me and say "No no. First you must do this". And every time I finished doing "This" she found something else for me to do. And just when I thought there could not possibly be anymore "This" and "That's", she said, "We stop now for Chow!". And she phoned out to have a meal delivered. I have to admit that it was one of the best Chinese meals I have ever tasted, but I was still keen to get started, and by now it was getting on for 6.30. Pinning Lilly down was like trying to nail a Blamonge to the ceiling.

When we got back on the bed, I remembered the last "That" and started from there, totally unaware that Lilly seemed to possess an armoury of "This" and "That's" - with a couple of others in reserve for good measure. At last, just before 9, I was allowed to bring down the final curtain on what, for me, had been a marathon - and it felt like it. The last thing I remember was the clock said 9.30, the next was the clock saying 6.30, with Lilly sleeping peacefully beside me.

Now, the reason I *had* to include Lilly is because she really did change my attitude towards the fair sex. I think that, prior to meeting her, I had probably been a little chauvinistic and cavalier with the Ladies. I now realised that they were also quite complex creatures, and that romance and slapped faces were all part of the complexity.

Lilly, you were an education - you certainly taught me a lesson.

HMS Cavalier 1959 - 1960   Memories Are Made Of This

Sunday Morning Divisions on Hong Kong quay side

I cannot leave Cavalier without mentioning one of Cavalier's more colourful characters - Lieutenant Telfer, the ships doctor who, when not lecturing the Crew on the advantages of condoms or supping Pink Gins, could be found wandering the upper deck, smartly dressed, with a two foot long, inflated pink plastic Elephant tucked under his arm. And, because he was so well respected, no one had the courage to ask what was the significance of the toy and, even today, it still remains a mystery to me.

Now our eighteen months were up, and it was time to get ready for home. I had a bran new uniform tailored and my gold badges and medal ribbon sewn on. I also had a long white silk ribbon on the front instead of the usual Navy Blue. In a couple of weeks time I was getting married and I wanted to look the part. My two best mates, Chas Bourne and Joe Loveday would be at the wedding with the latter as my best man. This time, we would be flying by Jet - and it would not take four days.

End of Commission - Reading the Wedding Banns

"Do you hear there. Those who have not yet done so, but who wish to, may now do so".

Advertisement

The GREY FUNNEL STEAM AND GENERAL NAVIGATION COMPANY announce the sailing of their luxury ship CAVALIER on an extended cruise leaving Singapore 24th June, 1960. (Air passage from the British Isles at no extra charge).

H.M.S. CAVALIER

Sailing for extended cruise June 24th, 1960

The Company's Officers are always at your disposal with advice on matters onboard or to assist you with your leisure ashore.

Early booking is essential at the Companys office at Haslemere, Hants.

The last picture of the 59/60 Commission crew

(I should have gone to Specsavers)

HMS Cavalier 1959 - 1960　　　　　　　　　　　　　　　　　　Memories Are Made Of This

And Finally. . . . .

Pants made by Vicki's Mum

Lola who I met in Hong Kong

Arriving North Malaya

Singapore Tea Party

MFV Trip

"Jock" Ross

Another Good Swim

One For The Road

Stand Easy

The Royal Naval hospital Haslar in Gosport and built in the mid 1700's, had served the Navy well, enjoyed a fine reputation, and was rated as possibly one of the top five hospitals in the Country. Although in my day it was generally reckoned that, no matter what illness or ailment you had when you entered the hospital, the treatment was *always* the same - Wire Brush and Paraffin.

Recently, there have been a number of news items stating that the Government had ear marked the hospital for closure, and I was reminded of a Navy myth concerning that establishment.

Apparently, the Queen was visiting the hospital accompanied by most of the senior medical staff, and she stopped at the bed of an old Sailor who was lying to Attention. The Queen asked the Sailor what was wrong with him and, much to the embarrassment of the staff, he replied, "Boils on me bum, your Majesty".

After the Queen had departed, the senior staff gave the old Sailor a thorough dressing down for his improper language and conduct in the presence of Her Majesty.

Anyway, and as chance would have it, a few weeks later, the Prince of Wales visited the hospital and, by coincidence, stopped at the same old Sailor's bed and asked what was ailing him. Noticing the threatening glares he was getting from the senior staff, the Sailor replied, "Boils on me b-b-body, sir".

The Prince looked slightly puzzled, and turning to the Senior Surgeon asked, "What treatment are you giving this chap? They seem to have spread since my Mother was here".

Now it's time to tie the knot . . . . .

RNH Haslar

Memories Are Made Of This

HMS President

1960 - 1961

'When at anchor here I ride, my bosom swells with pride'
W S Gilbert

Tied Up

I got to Vicki's and had a wonderful welcome home, and discovered that the wedding plans were just about complete, and that the wedding was all arranged for the following Saturday.

On the morning of the wedding I received a letter which, from the envelope, I could tell would be my next draft. I took it outside to read, opened it cautiously, read it and then folded it neatly and placed it in my wedding uniform pocket. It would keep for later.

Vicki's Mum and Dad had done us proud for the wedding, and we were able to hold the reception in the school hall.

When it came to the speeches I fumbled through mine trying to make sure I had not missed anyone on the Thank You list.

I then said that I had, that morning, received my next draft in the post and I withdrew the letter from my pocket.

I could see Vicki's face putting on a brave smile, she had been through this routine too many times before.

Then I announced that I was being sent to HMS President - both Chas and Joe gave out loud cheers and clapped because they knew what that meant - nine months working at the Admiralty in Whitehall.

And I ended by saying that consequently, on our return from honeymoon, we would be looking for a flat in the Stockwell area. I could see the light slowly dawning on Vicki's face, and the Navy could not have given us a nicer Wedding Present.

For the Honeymoon, I had hired a cabin cruiser on the Norfolk Broads and, for the next two weeks, I felt like the Captain of my own ship, with a very well disciplined crew and, with my Navigation skills, I could plot the time of arrival to a Pub to the nearest minute.

Just Married

'Sign 'ere, Lad'

HMS President 1960 - 1961　　　　　　　　　　　　　　　　Memories Are Made Of This

Wedding Album

Admiralty

That night we stayed at the Great Eastern Railway Hotel so that we could catch a train the following morning for the Norfolk Broads. It was not until we were in bed that we both realised how much confetti we had been carrying and, I am afraid, we left the room in a bit of a mess.

I loved the Broads, and here I was Captain of my own boat with a very disciplined crew, and I loved plotting a course for the next Pub and calculating the Time of Arrival. I knew that Vicki was a good cook from previous meals at home but, on the Broads in a small galley, she excelled and I was in unadulterated heaven.

On our return from the Broads, we quickly found a basement flat a short distance from the schoolhouse and, with some paint, wallpaper and the rest of my leave, we soon turned it into our first home.

Vicki's family had a small 49 cc moped which I learned to ride and, with a Provisional License, I had excellent transport from Stockwell to Whitehall and back

At Admiralty, you travelled in civilian clothing. And changed into half working gear and half Civvy gear, jumpers, sweaters and cardigans.

A draft to Admiralty was considered a Privilege and lasted for a maximum of nine months, and there was extra money for working in London.

For a young pair of Navy newly weds it was ideal.

In the Admiralty there were no radios, receivers or transmitters. Everything was handled by Teleprinters. The long distance Teleprinter channels, London to Singapore, were linked by radio but the transmitters were miles away and nothing to do with us. Neither did you have to sit at a keyboard and type the message, they were all punched onto lengths of paper tape. The tape would then be used to transmit the message and, at the other end, the Teleprinter would print the message and create a duplicate tape which could be used for relaying the message onwards.

Consequently I was in a brand new communications world and, fascinated, I had to know all about it. I ended up in the Tape Relay Centre as the "Snags Bosun" with the task of sorting out any bloomers and mistakes. It was a very powerful position, I had my own Tape Relay address so that I could be sent and send messages.

Within nine months I was an expert, and later this was to pay big dividends.

One evening on the twelve hour night shift, the duty Officer called me in for a chat and to see how I was getting on. He asked me if there was anything he could do for me. I replied, a bit hesitantly, that my nine months were almost up, and that I would love a Foreign Married Accompanied draft abroad. "Where to he asked?". Anywhere I replied.

Four days later he called me in again to say that, he had got me a married draft to Malta, but that I would be attached to the NATO contingent and, as such, would be entitled to duty free cigarettes, booze, petrol and, if I could afford it, a car. Would that be alright? - That will do nicely, thank you, sir.

Stand Easy

Time for a break and some more fiction. I received this one from my second ex wife, Joyce, and just had to include it - but I wouldn't want any one to think that our divorce is on the rocks.

Those that go down to the sea in ships.

A young woman, down on her luck, decided to end it all one night by casting herself into the cold, dark waters of Portsmouth Harbour.

As she stood on the edge of the dock, pondering her fate, a young sailor noticed her as he strolled by.

"You're not thinking of jumping, are you?". he jokingly asked.

"Yes, yes I am." replied the sobbing girl.

Putting his arm around her, the kind sailor coaxed her back from the edge.

"Look, nothing's worth that. I tell you what; I'm sailing off for Australia tomorrow. Why don't you stow away on board and start a new life over there. I'll set you up in one of the lifeboats on the deck, bring you food and water every night, and I'll look after you if you ' look after' me."

The girl, having no better prospects agreed, and the sailor snuck her on board that night. For the next 3 weeks the sailor would come to her lifeboat every night, bringing food and water and making love to her until dawn.

Then, during the fourth week, the captain was performing a routine inspection of the ship and it's lifeboats. He peeled back the cover to find the startled young woman and demanded an explanation.

The young woman came clean; "I've stowed away to get to Australia. One of your sailors is helping me out. He set me up in here and brings me food and water every night, and, and ....he's screwing me".

"He certainly is Miss", replied the Captain, "This is the Isle of Wight Ferry."

Now it's time to catch a 'plane for Malta, and two and a half years with the NATO Staff. . . . .

Memories Are Made Of This

HMS Phoenicia

1961 - 1963

'Twas for the good of my country that I should be abroad'
George Farquhar

Malta

I think both Vicki and I were excited, but her Mum and Dad soon realised that they would not be seeing their little girl again for two and a half years. The plan was for me to go out first and, as soon as I found somewhere to live, Vicki would fly out and join me.

As soon as the plane touched down in Malta, I got that 'I'm home' feeling again - I guess I just loved the place. I was housed in HMS Phoenicia, a shore establishment on Manoel Island, which was originally built by the Crusaders as part of the harbour defences.

As I walked back down the Road to get off the island, I had to pass the WooHa's old mooring bay and, without a Minesweeper to be seen, I would get a bit of lump in my throat and tended to refer to that period as 'The Old Days'. I reported to the NATO Headquarters situated in Florianna, where I was issued with my NATO Badge and Duty Free coupons for Cigs', booze and petrol. I did not have a car but I was determined to have one.

Most of the Navy lads who had their wives with them lived in the Sliema area. I wanted to be away from this area and, eventually, found a nice little flat in St Julian's for £7 a month. It was right on the sea front, and when you opened the bedroom shutters you had an unrestricted view of the beach and St Julian's Bay. The Land Lady was a lovely elderly widow whose husband had been a Doctor. Her name was Mrs. Briffa, and later we would become great friends - she reminded me of Mrs. Evans in Tredegar.

Before Vicki arrived I bought her a washing machine and a sewing machine and, with all these girlie comforts installed, patiently waited for her to join me about a month later. It was great having her out there with me and, over the two and a half year period, her parents came out and stayed with us and, during the summer school holidays, her younger sister Jennifer came and stayed - she loved the beach.

We also had a couple of visits from "Jock" Ross and Chas Bourne when there current ships visited Malta.

Just round the corner from the flat was a bar called the Swan which became my local. It was run by a dear old lady who, no matter how late it was, would never close until the last person had gone. We were totally accepted by the Maltese locals, and assimilated into their kind of life style quite easily.

One of the locals was always coming in and would generously give everyone packet after packet of cigarettes. I found out later that he was the local Customs Officer. I was beginning to love this lifestyle and I was picking up a few words in Maltese.

Two streets away was another bar called the Nappa where, on a Sunday night, three Mandolin and two Guitar players would meet and play beautiful Neapolitan music. Sometimes you could hear the music where we were living, and I loved going there with Vicki but, because one of the mandolin players was the barman, if you wanted a drink, you had to get it yourself.

On Manoel Island was a big NAAFI and Social Club. With advice from Mrs. Briffa, which was always available, we tended to buy most of our food from the local Maltese shops and traders, and we visited the Social Club whenever they had a Rock 'n Roll evening. Within a couple of months, I had found and bought my first car - a Hillman Minx saloon, and soon Vicki and I had just about explored every part of the Island.

Our favourite spot was Marfa in the north of the Island. It was barren and rocky but the sea was clear and blue, and you had a wonderful view across to Comino and Gozo. This then was how we were going to live for the next two and a half years, and we needed to make the most of it because we would never have it this good again.

HMS Phoenicia 1961 - 1963 　　　　　　　　　　　　　　　　　　　Memories Are Made Of This

Living in Malta

Lower Victoria Terrace. The view from the Bedroom window

Night time Bar-B-Q on the beach

Relatives visiting from England

My old Bar is now a shop

The Nappa still going strong

Driving In Malta

Although I had taken a few driving lessons in the Father in Law's car back home, I still needed a few more before I could feel confident enough to take a test. So I took myself off to the British School of Motoring, (BSM), on Sliema front.

Now, in order to avoid the laws of libel I need to make it quite clear that, to the best of my knowledge, the *Maltese* BSM is not and has never ever been either related to, or affiliated with, the *British* BSM.

Having signed on for five lessons, I was then taken to an open space behind the office where I was introduced to my driving Instructor, and their fleet of three badly battered and war torn Morris Minor 1000's.

The instructor invited me to get into the drivers seat of one and, as I did so, I noticed that there was no floor carpets, just bare, rusty metal with one or two holes and an occasional spot weld.

On the other hand, it did start, and the Instructor seemed to be quite pleased with that. We then spent the next hour in the yard reversing between two oil drums.

By the the fifth lesson I felt confident enough to take the test. At that time, the tests were conducted by the Police, and, as I somehow managed to finish the course outside the Policeman's house, I passed.

Looks Familiar

Maltese Rush Hour 1962

Driving On The Shady Side Of The Road

Alternative Transport

Driving in Malta

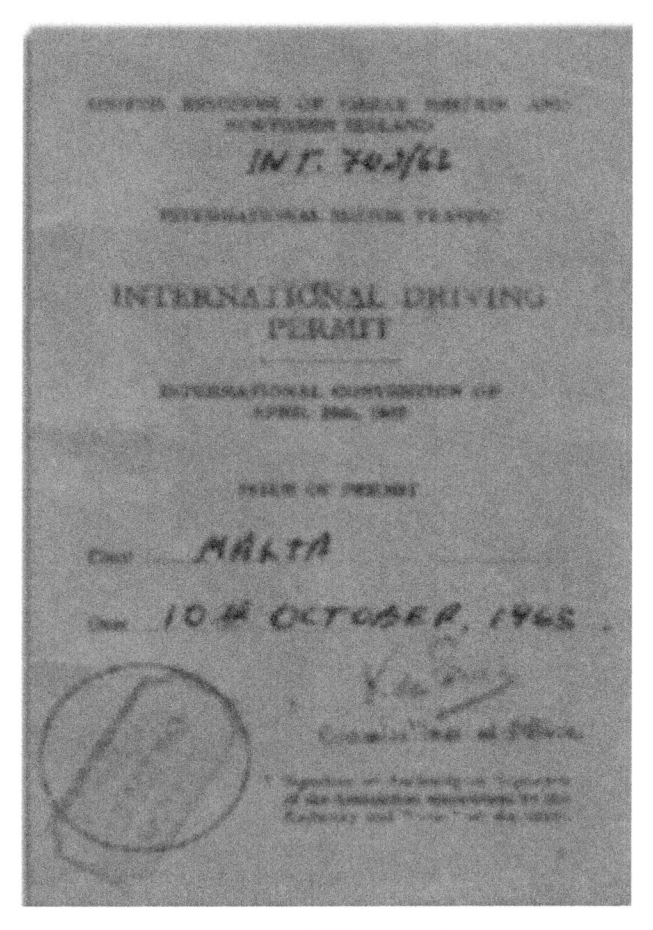

Super petrol was two shillings and two pence a gallon, and Regular Cost one shilling and ten pence a gallon. So for five Shillings, (25p today), I could buy two gallons of Super, two shots of Redex and still leave a generous tip!

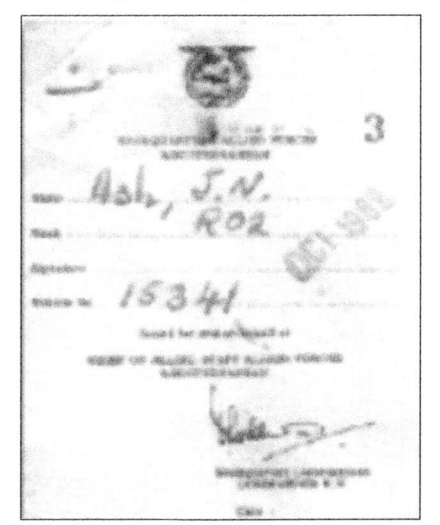

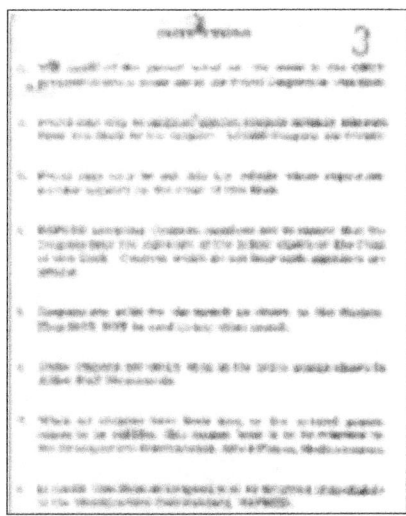

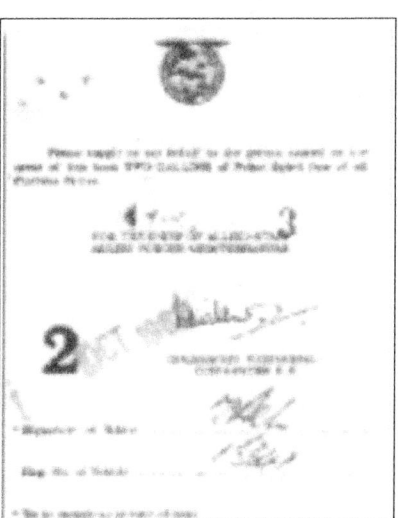

NATO Petrol Coupons

NATO Staff

For the whole of my stint in Malta I became very disappointed with the Navy. The NATO staff consisted of various naval ranks from NATO counties and, all told there was probably about fifteen of us. Working with me at the Communications Centre was two Turkish Chief Petty Officers and an Italian Petty Officer and, although there was a NATO communications room, they put Navy chaps in charge of it who were far junior to the Turkish and Italian chaps. And they had a right go at me on my first shift when I walked in wearing my NATO badge - I was forbidden to wear it. To me it smacked of juvenile pettiness, and completely negated the idea of trying to get various Navies to work together. My duty free cigarettes, booze, and petrol, plus the fact that I had a fairly decent car also seemed to cause a fair amount of friction and envy. However, I prefer to think that it was the people that were there at the time, rather than the Navy, who were to blame.

From then on in, I kept the cigarettes etc at home, and parked the car where it could not cause offence. I also tended to spend more time with the NATO people, and one in particular, Adil, a Turkish Chief Petty Officer and I became great friends. His wife was learning English at one of the Navy schools, and he wanted to learn as well but without going to school. In two years I had him swearing with the best of us, but he always used to complain to me that when he and his wife had a conversation in English, they could never understand each other - I wasn't a bit surprised.

Meanwhile in the 'Comcen' I became a Ship Shore operator. Now instead of sending signals from a ship, I was now receiving them on shore. They would then be passed on to the appropriate addressee's via the Teleprinter networks. I felt good having a Morse Key in my hand again and, as there was not much Navy traffic, I always called the Merchant ships that I could hear calling the UK and offer to relay their signals free of charge. The furthest distance I recorded was taking a message from the Kistna Dan in the Antarctic.

Sometime during this period I went on a six weeks course for the next exam that, if passed would take me to the next rank up - Leading Telegraphist or, as we were now being called, Leading Radio Operator. I breezed through the first four weeks course and the exams. The last two weeks was an intense course on Tape Relay Procedures and, looking at the faces around me, I could tell that none of them even knew what it meant. I was even surprised to find the Instructor having some difficulty. I kept quiet. but I knew I had done well in the exam. When the results came back, most of them were in the sixty to seventy percent range. My exam paper was dropped on my desk with the Instructor saying 'You know your Tape Relay Ash' - it was one hundred percent and had never been done before. My period as Snags Bosun at Admiralty had paid dividends and, although I did not know it at the time, my exam mark would eventually pay another dividend.

The only other thing that comes to mind in Malta at that time was, would you believe, being told to take a swimming test. I was furious, and felt that I had been slandered. To make it worse the test was to take place in one of the creeks where the water ranged from bracken to foul. I complained that I did not want to swim in foul water, but was ordered to do so. I noticed a couple of large rocks jutting a couple of feet above the surface about fifteen yards further down to my right. So with a sigh I said "OK Chief, here I go" and dived in. I let myself sink to the bottom, turned sharp right and swam underwater, knowing he could not see me, until I felt the rocks. I came slowly to the surface on the far side and stopped for a couple of minutes. He was frantically shouting my name at the water, and I was able to walk right up behind him without his noticing. So I tapped him on the shoulder and said "Did I pass?". The look of relief on his face was a picture, and he was never going to ask me to take another test.

A Dad Elect

One evening in Malta, Vicki and I were invited to a party with some friends of ours, and we were getting ready to go. As Vicki came out of the bathroom, made up and wrapped in a towel, I just could not help myself - so I did.

That evening at the party, I kept noticing that Vicki had an extraordinary calm and serene look about her. I had *never* seen this before, and I did not say anything, but I knew for certain that something was happening. So, when a couple of weeks later she informed me that she might be pregnant, I was not in the least bit surprised and, as far as I was concerned there was no 'might' about. It.

Although we had not planned to start a family, I was really pleased. And when it was confirmed by the Navy Medics, we wrote home to tell the parents, and I got a great deal of pleasure in addressing the envelopes to "Nanny and Grandad Elect". For the first six months, Vicki had the usual pregnancy symptoms but she did not look pregnant until about the sixth month and, at this time, even I could feel the faint movements coming from inside. We were now getting near the end of our two and half year stint, and we decided that now would be the best time for Vicki to fly home before the pregnancy got any further down the line.

After Vicki had left, the flat seemed empty but, with Mrs. Briffa for company and looking after me, and the amount of packing that needed to be done, I was too busy to be lonely. Mrs. Briffa was a wonderful women and my second Mrs. Evans from Tredegar. She was deeply religious, loved her Church and her faith but would never try to push it on to me, and neither did she criticise or comment on my atheist attitude towards religion. We would often sit in her kitchen, and she would tell me about some of her life's experiences which, had I been a believer, I would have to call Miracles. Her wartime memories of the Siege, the food shortages, the bombing and receiving the George Cross filled me with admiration. She also told me, with a look of triumph on her face, that she had prayed and lit a candle some months ago for Vicki to have a baby - now that's what I call Candle Power.

One Day, Mrs. Briffa made a spaghetti and invited me for lunch. The Maltese name for the spaghetti was literally translated as Dirty Spaghetti because everything they had went into it. It was a trifle over the top for my taste so, the following Saturday we started concocting our own recipe and, after a couple of Saturdays we had it to the point of perfection. I said to her, "Mrs Briffa, I still think there is something missing", and I went back into the flat and picked up a bottle of wine. I took the cork out and ran it around the inside the cooking pot, gave the pot a stir and tasted it with a cry of eureka. I then discovered that Mrs. Briffa also liked a glass of wine or two with her spaghetti. Even today, I still like to get out the big pot and make the odd spaghetti exactly the same way as we did on then - including the cork.

On another occasion she approached me a little nervously and, knowing that I could get duty free spirits, she asked if it would be possible for me to get her a bottle of brandy - she wanted it for medicine for her and her sister, and I said I would see what I could do. Now this was a difficult one, if you were caught selling your duty free rations you could have the privilege stopped for everyone. Anyway, I got her a litre bottle of 'Napoleon' for which she offered me money. I told her in a very stern voice, "Mrs Briffa, you told me this was for medicine and, in England, all medicines are free". Mrs. Briffa had the sense to know that I should not have done it, but she was very grateful and I was pleased that I had been able to do something for her.

On the 20th of June 1963 I said farewell to Mrs. Briffa and Malta, I was flying home with eight weeks leave to look forward to, and I was missing Vicki and the little lump she had taken with her.

Stand Easy

Wooha and HMS Shavington

HMS Cavendish refuelling

Let me pause for a moment before flying home for another fictitious story but, before I do, let me explain the science and thinking behind a naval manoeuvre referred to as a 'Jack Stay Transfer'.

This is when two ships steam parallel to each other, at a distance of some thirty to forty feet. A couple of lines are then passed from one ship to the other and secured. Then, with the use of a pulley and line, it becomes possible to pass items from one ship to the other. Items usually consists of things like Mail or stores, but can also include homo sapiens.

The picture shows a member of the Wooha's crew being transferred to a Minesweeper, HMS Shavington, with both ships travelling in parallel at about eight knots.

It therefore follows that the success, or otherwise, of this operation depends to a large extent on the skills of the people steering the ships. Get too close and the lines go slack, and the package dips into the water. Too far apart and the lines will snap, and you lose the package.

This story, which I heard after I had left the Navy, concerns an Aircraft Carrier that was carry out one of these manoeuvres with a naval Tanker, taking onboard both stores and fuel.

The Tanker Captain, using a megaphone, called across to the Carrier asking if they had a Catholic Padre on board. The Captain of the Carrier replied that they had, and how could he be of service to them. The Tanker informed the Carrier that it was Sunday and that they had not had a church service since leaving Port, and would it be possible for him to come across and perform a short Service. To which the Carrier Captain agreed.

Now, as the lines were being set up, the Padre came up onto the Carriers flight deck and, knowing what he was about to do, gingerly looked over the side at the water flowing like the Colorado rapids between the two moving vessels.

An old sailor, who just happened to be standing close by at the time, noticed the look of distress and discomfort on the Padre's face. So the sailor approached the Padre and, putting a comforting arm around his shoulder, said, "Cheer up Padre. Just think, if you'd had two more years seniority, you could have walked across".

Now it's time to catch that 'plane for home. . . . .

Memories Are Made Of This

HMS Murray

1963 - 1964

'A life on the ocean wave, a home on the rolling deep'
Samuel J Arnold

First Born

When I arrived home from Malta, Vicki looked well and truly pregnant, calm and serene. However, when we got into bed that night she seemed a bit shy because she thought that her stomach looked big and ugly. I thought it looked great and, when I put my ear against it, I could hear both Vicki's and the babies heart beats. In this position I could also receive a fairly powerful kick in the head. I was mesmerised. This was life and this was my baby, I could not see it, but I could certainly hear and feel it.

Vicki was taken into hospital while I was on leave. I spent what was to become my 'Longest Day' sitting in the kitchen waiting for the phone to ring, and her Dad popping in every five minutes. Eventually the call came through in the late afternoon - it's a Girl. It's a Girl?

My emotions were strangely mixed. It was all over, Vicki and the baby were both fine but, the name I had chosen, Steven Christopher, and the small fishing rod I had made for it were now both obsolete. Somehow, throughout the whole pregnancy, it had *never* occurred to me that it might be a girl - but I just had to go and see it.

In the hospital Vicki looked fine but a little tired and, as we were talking, the nurses wheeled in all the babies and placed them alongside the appropriate beds. It was unadulterated bedlam. They were all bawling their hearts out except for mine, she was fast asleep. I was truly impressed. I wanted to pick her up but she looked so small, frail and peaceful, I did not dare touch her. A week later, that at the time seemed like an age, I had Vicki and the baby home. During the week I had decided on Susan Christine for the name - it was as near as I could get to Steven Christopher.

For the first two weeks all I could do was stand and stare, and took every opportunity to see Susan in her cot. I wanted to pick her up but I was so frightened of hurting her. I did manage to get her to grasp my finger while she was being fed, and I could not believe how small a babies hand could be and still contain five fingers. I was in a new world, and one for which the Navy had not trained and prepared me.

At that time, we were living with Vicki's parents at the schoolhouse and needed to find a place of our own. We found a small ground floor flat with a double bedroom on Knights Hill in West Norwood. It definitely was not the style of living that we had become accustomed to in Malta, but we did have a fair size garden at the back, and a big cellar in which I could ferment my home made wine. On the floor above were two retired ladies who took an instant liking to Susan.

By the end of my leave, Susan had put on weight and was progressing nicely. We had the flat sorted out as best we could, and it was not too far from either Vicki's or my parents homes - it was now time to turn my attention to my next draft. Surprise bloody surprise, guess where?

Here's a clue.

HMS Hardy

Portland Again

Portland is a miserable, cold place at the best of times, and this was mid August 1963 - and still some years before the Government gave us Global Warming. I suppose I had got use to the Mediterranean sunshine and climate, and this made the place seem even more miserable.

Now, Dear Reader, if you are thinking that you have been here previously and read that bit somewhere before, and you are feeling bored with it the second time round - Good! Because that is exactly how I felt at the time. Here I was, after another trip to the Maltese climate, back in bloody Portland and 140 miles from Vicki and Susan. HMS Murray, as with HMS Dundas, was a new type of frigate, and the English Channel at Portland seemed to delight in giving her the roughest passage possible but, this time, I was *never* sea sick! I had been promoted to Leading Radio Operator, and Vicki had sewn my new badges beautifully onto all my uniforms.

One of my jobs was to switch on the ships Radio Broadcast system. This was invariably the BBC Home Service, and it was Tannoyed through out the ship. I used to make sure everyone heard the Shipping Forecast, and I loved it when they spoke those three magic words, "Dover, Wight, Portland". And, if it was followed by something like, "South Westerly, force five to six", I knew that, anything above a Force 5, and I was going to get an extra dinner and, possibly, somebody else's rum.

The first time at sea on the Murray, I could feel the ship being tossed around and waited expectantly for the first sign of queasiness and, when after an hour, I still had not felt sick, I had to go on the upper deck to check that it was rough. And it was, and I felt good, but I still could not believe it so, for a final check, I went to the stern of the ship. (When you are sick at sea that is the place to be). And yes, sure enough, there were a dozen or so of the younger members of the crew, standing with their backs to the wind, their heads hung well over the rails and getting covered in spray. I said to them, "Don't worry about it lads, I have just seen the Chef and, for lunch, he has made a lovely thick Pea soup, with bits of Pork Chop fat floating in it", and, as they all spewed in unison, I thought to myself, 'Yep, definitely two dinners today'.

The Weekend leave was the same as it had been on Dundas. And every time I arrived home Susan seemed to be twice as big as she was the on the previous occasion, her rate of growth amazed me. Now I could hold her and sit her on my lap, and I loved it when she started crawling all over me - I could not get enough of her. Round about April 1964, Vicki surprised me with the news that she was pregnant again, and although it was not going to be easy, I was secretly pleased that I would see this pregnancy all the way through - including the home birth.

To my surprise, Murray had a trip to the Mediterranean for an exercise, and we called In at Malta. I was able to visit Mrs. Briffa who wanted to know everything about the new baby, and I think Susan is probably listed somewhere in her chronicle of candle curiosities. The Murray also paid a courtesy visit to Kiel and, as we travelled along the Kiel Canal, I noticed this time that the Germans seemed to be a little more friendly - but they *still* had the 1966 World Cup to come.

On the 24th of August 1964, having spent a year on the Murray, I was informed, out of the blue, that I was being drafted back to *Admiralty* and that I was to be the Supervisor of the Tape Relay Centre. Now I knew that with the Admiralty you only ever got one bite of the cherry, and I had already had mine. I had to conclude that this second bite was down to my exam results, and that they needed some specialist expertise for something.

I said my farewells to Murray, and caught a train for London, Vicki and and the baby, Susan.

Stand Easy

In order to go ashore in Portland, either to the local Pubs or into Weymouth, you had to pass through the Dockyard Gates. The gates were manned both day and night by naval police who were always on the lookout for items being smuggled out of the dockyard.

I was continually trying to find ways of getting a couple of extra packs of cigarettes out for the folks back home. This was usually done by travelling with a non smoking mate, and getting him to carry the extra packs.

That was my way of doing things but, as the following fiction reveals, there were other ways.

Dockyard gates at Portsmouth, and Jack is going ashore pushing a wheelbarrow with a huge cardboard box in it. Dockyard police stop and search the box but find nothing but polystyrene filling.

This continues for the next few nights. The Police are convinced that just one day, there is going to be some contraband in that box and they'll catch Jack red-handed.

After 21 days and the same routine nothing turns up and Jack's ship leaves Portsmouth.

A short while later, Dockyard Stores report 21 wheelbarrows missing.

Now, back to the story. . . . .

HMS Murray entering Grand Harbour, Malta

"Do you hear there. Liberty guys to glamorise. Fall in abaft the after smoke stack"

Memories Are Made Of This

HMS President

1964 - 1966

'Oh rest ye, brother mariners, for we shall not wander more'
Alfred, Lord Tennyson

Admiralty

After a Pint in the Silver Cross, I rejoined Admiralty on the 26th August 1964 and started 'Clock Watching'. I was due to leave the Navy in May 1966 and, consequently, I had only another twenty one months to serve. It occurred to me that if I spent the maximum nine months here, that there would still be enough time for them to send me back to Portland or somewhere similar - I could not take a third spell and, now, there was not enough time left to take Vicki *and* the family abroad. So, somehow, I had to find a way to make myself either indispensable or invisible. Believe it or not, the invisible bit turned out to be the easiest.

On my first watch I reported to the Chief of the Watch who, at that very moment, had a problem. A new machine had been installed, and he needed someone to man it and it *had* to be a volunteer. Curious as to what it could be, I said I would do it. He took me to a door, which looked like a broom cupboard and opened it. Inside was a lift cage. He told me to press the Down button, and at the bottom would be someone to meet me. Now, as we were already in the basement of the Admiralty, I expected it to go down one or possibly two floors - was I in for a surprise. The lift started its downward journey and, when I heard a Tube Train rumble past *above* my head, I began to realise why it had to be a volunteer. At the bottom I was staggered. I was in a maze of illuminated Tube size tunnels with signposts to various places in London. I was met by another Leading Radio Operator who showed me into a large area which, during the war, had been the Trafalgar Switchboard. I had heard of it but never dreamed that I would ever see it. Standing in the middle of the room was a big metal box, about the size of a Ford Transit Van, making a humming noise. It had a notice on it which read:

> **"Das computin machine is nicht fer gittin yer fingure poken an pickin, else der fuseboxen ict is spitten an sparkin"**

Even down here there was Navy humour to be found. I was then taken over to a desk with what today would be called a Console. It was basically a box with various lights and a keyboard. I was intrigued and had to know more.

The big box was indeed a computer consisting mainly of a massive magnetic drum. Now instead of the messages being sent from Teleprinter to Teleprinter, they were routed to the computer which would then send them to the appropriate addressees Teleprinters. If you can imagine today's Internet E-mail system without a screen, you will have a good idea of what we had here - and this was 1964. My job would be to watch the lights on the Console to make sure that the traffic was flowing smoothly, check the odd message that the computer threw out because it had nowhere to send it and, most important of all, check the drum storage capacity. When it reached eighty five percent full, you signalled the stations to stop transmitting until it had reduced to a safe level.

I then discovered that we had a similar machine in one of the corners of our far flung Empire, which could reach all our Far East stations including Australia. And when I found that their machine was connected to ours, it began to dawn on me that I was in charge of the Navies latest Hi-Tech communications system and, having previously spent some time as the Snags Bosun, anything the machine threw out was easy to deal with. After about a week, the lad that had shown me around left the Navy at the end of his engagement, and I took over. I was in my element and, down here, I was virtually invisible.

Susan Christine Ash

Now, I would like to digress for a moment to expound a Social Sciences theory, which I have concocted and concluded from my own conducted researches.

It is well known that most females can twist a man round their little finger, and I always imagined that this was due to either an idiosyncratic gene with which they were naturally born or, more likely, something they learnt from their Mothers.

Wrong on both accounts!

I discovered that when a three to four year old daughter climbs up on to your lap, throws her arms round your neck, looks you in the eye, smiles, gives you a big, wet, slobbering kiss and then starts the conversation with something like, "Dad, do you think ....?", you know straight away, before she can even get the words out, that you have already surrendered, capitulated, acquiesced *and* given in - in fact, you have already started to say "Yes".

Now, of course, when they come to realise the power of persuasion they have with this modus operandi, they carefully nurture and carry it with them through out the rest of their lives.

And the first fella they meet in later years is nothing less than a Lamb to the slaughter.

It really grieves me to say this, Gentleman, but I am afraid I *have* to blame the Dads and, trust me, I share and feel your shame, guilt and pain just as much as you do.

Susan starting to toddle at Chertsey Camp site

Look where you're going! Head up! Shoulders back! Chest out! Left, Right, Left, Right

Dad, do you think. . . . . .

Janet Caroline Ash

I did not know it at the time, but 1965 was going to be a good year.

Vicki was pregnant with the new baby due at any moment. Susan was crawling all over the house and over me. One day we lost her. We searched the flat, the cellar and various cupboards. In the end I went upstairs to where the two elderly retired ladies lived, to find Susan sitting with them at a table. I think the relief on both Vicki's and my faces must have been worth a photograph. I did not want to dampen Susan's spirit of adventure but we thought that, in this case, a stairway gate was essential.

The pregnancy was going well but seemed to be taking ages. We both agreed that we would have a Home Birth and, as this was another area in which the Navy had failed miserably to train and prepare me, I spent some time at the local Library.

In January, we lodged Susan with my Mum and Dad. Vicki went into Labour, and was attended to by a mountain of a midwife. The Midwifes first words to me were, "Don't look so worried Mr. Ash, I have done this before and I have never yet lost a Father". If that was supposed to comfort me - it didn't! She placed an Oxygen bottle on the bed and, I think, I spent more time on the receiving end of it than Vicki. When the baby was born, the midwife wrapped it up and handed it to Vicki saying, "There you are Mr. Ash, you have a beautiful baby daughter". I had watched the *whole* of the birth and had not even noticed what sex the baby was - that Oxygen was good stuff.

This time I was not going to make the same mistakes that I had made when Susan was born. I had no preconceived ideas this time about the sex, (even though I still had the fishing rod), and although I would like to have had a son, I consoled myself with the thought that, in fifteen or so years time, I would be completely surrounded with Panties and Bra's - and that should be enough for any man of that age.

Finding the name Steven Christopher was now totally redundant, we had the new baby Christened Janet Caroline. The Janet bit came easily but we could not think of a suitable middle name. However, in those days, there were wonderful Pirate Radio Stations in the North Sea, and both Vicki and I loved listening to Radio "Caroline" - so that solved that little problem. As this was my second time round, I felt far more confident picking up Janet and holding her, but I still could not get over how small a babies hand can be. And it was not long before I could sit with her on one arm and have Susan crawling all over me - I loved it.

Janet's Christening with Vicki's Mum

Defaulters

Meanwhile, some hundred odd feet beneath Nelson's Column, the computer and I were getting on like a pair of old shipmates, but I had been there for seven months and I started to worry about my nine months coming to an end. When not on watch I was at home, and I could see the two girls growing well. Susan had started walking and talking, and both girls seemed to vie with each other for my attention - I could not be parted from them now. Then something so miraculously well timed happened that, afterwards, I had to put it down to another one of Mrs. Briffa's patent catholic candles.

One afternoon shift we were all told that we had to go to a certain room at a certain time, and my appointment was for about 3.30. When I arrived in the room, there was a Medical Officer with the rank of Commander and a Sick Bay rating. I was ordered to sit in a chair and open my mouth. He had not introduced himself, but it was becoming apparent that he specialised in dentistry. After a few prods, he turned to the Sick Bay chap and said, "Have this one in". I was then given a dental appointment and sent me on my way. Outside I dropped it in the rubbish bin - now I had to wait.

Sure enough, just as I had anticipated, four days later I arrived on shift to be told by the Chief of the Watch that I was on Defaulters. I was marched smartly up to the Officer of the Watch and told, "Off caps". The Chief then said in the customary military manner, "LRO Ash sir, charged with being absent from place of duty, namely, dental appointment, sir"

"What have you got to say for yourself, Ash?". asked the Officer of the Watch. I said that I could not recall making a dental appointment but, if I could retrieve my diary from next door I would then know how to plead. I was allowed to retrieve my diary knowing full well it did not contain anything, I just wanted a moment to rehearse what I was going to say next - this had to be better than any of my old school Christmas plays. "Well, Ash?". So I said that I had checked my diary and that I could safely say, without fear of contradiction, that "since I have been at the Admiralty, at no time during that period have *I* (emphasising the "I") ever made a dental appointment for *myself*"

I knew I was on safe and solid ground. When I was on the Cavalier, I had looked up the Rules and Regulations concerning medical treatment in a vain attempt to get my Junior out of a rather embarrassing medical examination. Basically what the Rules said was that no medical procedures could be carried out on a person without their permission. The days when they could use a Serviceman for medical experiments were long gone. And looking at the faces of both the Chief and the Officer, it was obvious they knew it too. "Case dismissed", said the officer. "On caps", said the Chief. "Permission to speak?". said I. "Yes, of course Ash. What is it?"., said the Officer in a far friendlier manner.

So I explained that I could take a joke and a skylark as well as any other but, with my record, I drew the line when it placed me on Defaulters. I then went on to say that I was now requesting an investigation, and that the appropriate disciplinary action be taken against the culprit (singular) and, in true Stripey Watson fashion, I continued to say that if I did not find the outcome satisfactory, I might want to take it further up the chain. I then checked to make sure that the Chief had logged every word. So, once again I had to wait - but not for long.

Within a week, the same Officer told me that there had been a "bit of a cock up with the names", which we *both* knew was not true. But then he went on to say in a circumnavigated way that, if I dropped the investigation, I would be able to see out my time at Admiralty. - *Yes!* The over zealous Dentist had dealt me a hand full of spades, and invisibility was no longer the Dress of the Day.

Tape Relay Centre

Round about the middle of 1965, I handed over the computer to another LRO, and took up my position as the Supervisor of the Tape Relay Centre. I had about nine people working for me - a mixture of Sailors and Wrens. I admired the latter, they had the same training that we were given and their typing skills were usually better than ours. They never flagged on the twelve hour night watch, and they could take a joke just as well as we could. I had a good team.

The biggest problem we had was when we received a tape for several addressees and the computer could not split it up into separate tapes for each address. One of the wrens would take the tape to a machine, sit down, and produce the appropriate number of copies. There were periods when we had so many of these tapes, that it caused quite a back log.

Anyway, the Army had now installed the same type of computer as we had, and they were connected to us so, out of curiosity, I said to the Wren, 'Bring one of those multi address tapes over here, but make sure all the addressees are Navy'. We then went over to the Army link and sent it to them - and it was not long before it started coming back. Both the Wren and I stood with our mouths agog as we received tape after tape each with a different single address on it. The Army computer had split it for us. So I said to her, 'Now you know what to do in the future', and she smiled. I knew of course that it would probably double the amount of traffic through the Army machine and, sooner or later, was bound to be noticed. But I thought I would sit back and wait for them to complain - they never did, and I put it down to one of the benefits and blessings of being both the Senior Service *and* part of the Elite.

All messages in and out of the Centre had to carry a unique identification number so that it could be checked and accounted for by the end of the day. However, as a Supervisor, I could send ZIFs. These were unnumbered messages sent on a Supervisor to Supervisor level, and were used for sorting out snags and bloomers, and they were never logged or recorded. One night shift there was a ZIF from the Supervisor at Portsmouth. Apparently he had read in the local paper about a five year old lad in hospital with leukaemia, who was not expected to live long enough to see Christmas, and all the lad wanted for Christmas was Christmas Cards. The ZIF contained the lad's name and hospital address, and ended with 'Can you do anything with this?'.

The ZIF was printed and pinned up on the notice board. It was then sent to every addressee in the UK, the Mediterranean, and then via our Computer to the Far East stations. Now due to the shift patterns, I cannot say for certain what the outcome of this exercise was, but I seem to remember someone saying that the lad died shortly after. Sad, but it's a good example of the silent, unseen and unsung side of the Navy that I really loved.

In February 1966, with only three months left to serve, I recognised that it was fast approaching decision time. I was now a married man with a family of my own, and I had to start seriously thinking about the future. Signing on for a few more years was one option. I had also been thinking about joining the Diplomatic Wireless Service, that is where most of the Navy Radio Operators seem to end up. Somehow, with a family, neither of these two options appealed to me and. at the same time, I now had this yearning to somehow have a place of my own, somewhere in the suburbs where it was green. I needed my own piece of this blessed plot. But how?

That was the problem. In my last four weeks in the Navy I had either another piece of luck or, more likely, the last of Mrs. Briffa's candles.

Preparing For Civvy Street

If 1965 had been a good year for me, 1966 was going to be even better.

During the last three months of your Service, you are entitled to all sorts of leave, mainly to ease you into Civvy street. During this period I received a card from the National Association For The Employment of Regular Sailors, Soldiers And Airmen. Sounds impressive, but it is basically an authorised, none profit making recruitment agency. And the card invited me along for a chat, so I went.

The office was small and cramped. The chap sitting opposite me was obviously ex military and, after exchanging pleasantries, he asked me what I would like to do. I think that by now I had probably decided on the Diplomatic Wireless Service, and I started the conversation with the words, "Well, for the past two years I have been working with this computer and.." Before I could say anymore, he interrupted with, "Computers, Oh yes, that's the place to be these days. Excuse me a moment".

He then picked up the phone and spoke to someone who also sounded like a military man. When he put the phone down he said, "I have got you an interview with Don Rowland's at ICL for tomorrow afternoon. Can you attend?". - Of course I could.

This was my first venture into Civvy street. I did not know what to expect or how to conduct myself during an interview. I was met at reception by Don's Secretary and, as she led me upstairs to his office, we had to walk along a long passage way with a long glass wall.

I could not believe what I was seeing. Behind the glass wall was a massive room filled with computers and peripherals. There were chaps loading tape decks and running streams of paper tape through the fastest readers I had ever seen. By the time I got to Don's office I was gobsmacked - this interview *had* to go right

Don Rowland's was every bit a military man from his clothes down to his moustache, and I immediately took to him. Don was also familiar with the Official Secrets Act and stayed clear of asking me anything which would bring me into conflict with it.

It was a pleasant interview which ended by Don saying that I could start on the 23 rd of May, my leaving date, as a trainee Computer Operator, with a salary of £740 per annum - exactly the same as I was getting in the Navy.

Three days later I received a letter from ICL with my contract of employment detailing everything Don had said. I was to start on a three week training course at their establishment in Cookham, and then join one of the Four shifts at Bridge House South in Putney.

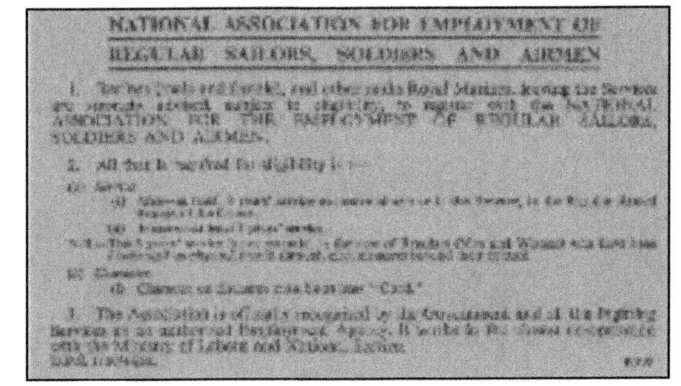

Stand Easy

Before leaving the Admiralty and the Navy, and for my final story, I would like to relate an incident that happened to one of the less popular Chiefs of the Watch.

This one would have been out of his depth in a Car Park puddle. He was the living embodiment of modified panic, tempered by the ability to pass the buck at the appropriate moment. Being fluent in Zanussi, he was about as useful as a cat flap in an elephant enclosure, and it seemed that his sole purpose in life was simply to serve as a warning to others.

In the Comcen he was completely lost, and only just got through each shift by being carried on the shoulders of the staff under him. Although slow and doddery, he was a stickler for security so that, when ever a classified signal, (that is a signal marked Restricted, Confidential or Secret), was put on his desk, he would put it in an envelope so that no one else could see it - even though it had been read by all. One day, a couple of the lads collected about a dozen Restricted signals and secreted them into his brief case. Now, this is how the rest of the story was related to me by some one on the night shift who had taken over from him.

Apparently, about an hour before midnight, the phone in the Comcen rang with this Chief on the other end saying that he had found a lot of confidential material in his brief case, and that he was returning to the Comcen by the most secure route - an Underground train. Fifteen minutes later the phone rang again. It was the Chief saying that, for security reasons, he had decided to change trains at every Station, and that he was now at such and such and would phone again at the next station.

This procedure was repeated for the next five stations and, by now, the whole of the night shift, who had been informed about the brief case, were all sitting around the phone in hysterics. Then came the sixth call. He was now within three stations of Charring Cross but, unfortunately, the Tube had closed down for the night.

A Blast From The Past

During my terminal leave, I had to pay a visit to the Navy barracks at HMS Victory, Portsmouth, for my 'Decommissioning'. So last, but by no means least, a Naval Broadside from yesterday's Navy, aimed at today's Political Correctness aficionados:

Nelson: "Order the signal to be hoisted Hardy".

Hardy: "Aye, aye sir".

Nelson: "Hold on, that is not what I dictated to the Signals Officer. What is the meaning of this?"

Hardy: "Sorry, sir".

Nelson: (Reading aloud) "England expects every *person* to do their duty, regardless of *race*, *gender*, *sexual orientation*, *religious persuasion*, *age* or *disability*. Good grief, what gobbledygook is this?".

Hardy: "Admiralty policy, sir. We are now an equal opportunities Employer. We had the devil's own job getting 'England' past the sensors, lest it be considered racist".

Nelson: "Whatever happened to rum, sodomy and the lash?".

Hardy: "Rum is off the menu now, and there is a ban on corporal punishment, sir".

Nelson: "What about sodomy?".

Hardy: "Ah, I believe *that* is to be positively encouraged, sir".

Nelson: "In that case - kiss me Hardy".

Navy Anon

And *that*, Dear Reader, is where I secure from Action Stations, stop engines, drop anchor, pack my Kitbag, finish my Tot, take leave of my senses, plot a course and head for a well deserved Make and Mend.

Duty done.

Reflections

Now I could relax and enjoy the remainder of my leave and, as I looked around me, I began to notice how much the country had changed since the austere Fifties. There was no more Rationing. You could still find the odd bomb site, but they were all boarded up waiting for the developers to move in, ("Squat now while stocks last" became the contemporary slogan). A Horse and Cart were a rarity, and the Trams and Trolley Busses had all gone. The Clean Air Act had banished the old London Smog's, and coal was no longer fashionable. Nuclear Power promised 'Free Electricity' for everyone.

The average price of a house when I joined the Navy was about £500, (In 1953, 31 Walterton Road was sold for £400), now prices were in the three to four thousand pounds range.

The mainly American Rock 'n Roll era was beginning to fade, and being replaced by the Rolling Stones, the Beatles and other British talent. Pirate Radio Stations in the North Sea fed the latter to a keen and enthusiastic audience. In the mid fifties, the Bill Haley "Rock around the Clock" film caused cinema seats to be ripped out so that the audience could Rock 'n Roll in the aisles. Some bright spark took the idea a little further by inventing the Disco Dance venue, and the grand old Ballroom Halls that had been so popular during the war, like the Hammersmith Palais, started to die. The Friday afternoon school Ballroom Dance lessons now seemed to have been a waste of time and effort.

With the vehicle MOT test you could no longer buy an old banger from a bargain basement and drive It until it dropped, and the Mini Moke was the car to own. Motorways were beginning to scar the countryside. For the fellar's, flared trousers and kipper ties were a must, along with Sideburns and shoulder length hair. Lager was the beer to drink, followed by a Curry and, if you wanted to take a trip, you flew LSD.

The novel Lady Chaterley's Lover had "opened the floodgates", and Mary Whitehouse was fighting a losing battle with the Nations morals and the BBC. Suzie Wong, Christine Keeler and Mandy Rice-Davis were the Ladies with whom to be seen, and the Contraceptive Pill and Sliced Bread were competing with each other for the title of 'Eighth wonder of the world'.

The glory of the 1966 World Cup football match was just around the corner and, as if all these were not enough, a lovely lady, by the name of Mary Quant, had just invented the Mini Skirt - and, with some of the girls, it was difficult to tell where a skirt finished and a pellmet began.

Bob Dylan summed it all up nicely with his song, 'The times they are a changing'. It was the 23 rd of May 1966, and I was about to enter a bran new world as a Civvy - but, by heck, it looked and felt good.

31 Walterton Road

Mini, Micro or Pellmet?

Apologies

> To the people I cited
> Both living and dead:
> I have borrowed your words
> And now they are read.
>
> And if I misquoted,
> Or mis-spelt a name:
> Accept my regrets
> My errors - my shame.

I just want to sign off this Naval career section of my early life by saying that it has given me a fair amount of pleasure, (and some embarrassment), putting it on paper and, if in doing so, I have upset or offended any Feminists or Political Correctness buffs, I tender my unreserved apologies. My only excuse for having done so is that I lived through, and have written about, an age when one could call a spade a spade, and not just think so.

I would also like to tender my thanks to all those unsung heroes who have populated the Internet with their killer Navy web sites, they have been a source of both information and inspiration. And, although nostalgia is not what it used to be, the Ganges and Cavalier sites brought both a lump to my throat and a tear to my eye. And Rum Ration has had me in hysterics. Whoever you are, thank you.

However, writing does have it's downside. In addition to words like 'Dghajsas' causing my Spell Checker to give up the ghost, I have also experienced one or two frustrating moments, when I have vainly searched my thesaurus for domestic equivalents to use in lieu of Naval terminology and slang. In most cases no such synonym exists, (try entering 'Kye'). And, although the story tends to lose a little of it's flavour and humour without the customary colourful language, I feel sure that you, Dear Reader, will be able to grasp the gist of the narrative without asking for it to be decoded.

Whilst writing and searching through old photographs, documents and Web Sites, I was staggered by the number of subordinate reminiscences which came flooding back, far too many to mention. So I have restricted myself to those memories which, in my opinion, probably had the most profound influence on my life at that time. And to those that I have missed, but who would claim a part, again my apologies.

I think I also have to apologise for the condition of some of the photographs and documents that I have included. I am afraid that they, like me, have been ravaged, (or possibly ravished, thank you Lilly), by the passage of time.

So, in the sunset years of old age, (Old Age? That's when the candles cost more than the cake, and actions creak louder than words), I say farewell and best wishes to you, and leave you with this last parting thought;

"If I had my life to live again, I'd still make the same mistakes - only sooner"

Sunset, sir.

John N Ash, (AKA Jerry Hatrick) Leading Radio Operator February 14th 2016.

Appendix   Memories Are Made Of This

Index

	H.M.S. Ganges	Page 118
	H.M.S. Woodbridge Haven	Page 119
	Malta - The Gut	Page 120
	Suez	Page 121
	H.M.S. Cavalier	Page 122
	Malaysian Medal	Page 124
	Maldive Islands	Page 125
	My 70th Birthday	Page 126
	Naval Humour	Page 127

——————-ooOoo——————

Appendix 1 Memories Are Made Of This

HMS Ganges

One of the proudest moments in my life was when, after eighteen months of training, I left HMS Ganges as a fully trained Boy Telegraphist. Now, after seventy years of service, HMS Ganges has closed to make way for a massive Urban Development scheme. The 142 foot mast has been listed, and will remain on site.

The only part of Ganges still recognisable today is the Parade Ground, marked with an 'X', and the mast.

HMS Woodbridge Haven

HMS Woodbridge Haven spent her last years of service in the Far East, before sailing back to the UK in the early 1960's to be scrapped. However, whilst in Hong Kong, she seems to have been stitched up by the New Zealand Navy, as the following story indicates.

A 'DAUNTING' Experience

By Ray West (Ex-CPO Cox'n).

Old MS104 & MS108 hands will remember that the pennant number of HMS Woodbridge Haven was P58.

In early 1961 the 104th paid a visit to Hong Kong. This was just after the new basin had been opened, and Wooha was secured alongside with the New Zealand frigate Rotoiti on her outboard side. At the time, I was serving on HMS Fiskerton.

After leaving harbour on the way to Singapore, we took up station on Wooha's port side. After a short time, it was noticed from the bridge that the pennant numbers on her port side had been changed from P58 to F53.

Having been on Cyprus Patrol when Undaunted and Maxton collided off Larnaca, Cyprus, I remembered this was Undaunted's pennant number. After confirming this, our skipper, (Lt.Cdr R.D.D. Bamford RN), had to find a way of informing 'Captain IF' onboard the Wooha of his problem. After some consideration he had the following signal sent by light.

From Fiskerton
To Woodbridge Haven

"Are you 'Undaunted' on the starboard side as well?".

Consternation followed on Wooha's bridge. The Captain was seen to arrive, swiftly followed by the First Lieutenant. After some head-scratching, the Chief Bo's'uns Mate was seen to make his way to the bridge, swiftly followed by 'No1' and Buffer gazing over the port side at the pennant numbers.

Situation understood, the entire Squadron was brought to a halt whilst a doughty AB, or maybe two, went over the side on a stage and repainted the offending letter and figures.

HMS Undaunted F53   **HMS Woodbridge Haven P58**

Appendix 3　　　　　　　　　　　　　　　　　　　　　　Memories Are Made Of This

Malta - The Gut

The Gut today. A sad sight and hardly recognisable.

However, it is still possible to see some of the old Bar signs above the bricked up doorways of old haunts. But my two favourites signs, Dirty Dick's and the Egyptian Queen, are now no longer visible.

Today. Looking up the Gut

Suez

I found the following extract on the Suez web site. It was written by the Commanding Officer of HMS Aldington, one of the Minesweepers which accompanied HMS Woodbridge Haven to Port Said. HMS Aldington

By Lt Commander J.D.Hegarty. MNI. RN. (Rtd).

"The Suez Crisis" had materialised, and orders for Operation Musketeer came through. 108 Minesweeping Squadron was to combine with 104 Squadron, (which had arrived in Malta, from Harwich), for operations to support the landings at Port Said.

The HQ Ship, HMS Woodbridge Haven, would co-ordinate our efforts in this role.

Landing Day was to be 6th November 1956. Musketeer was a major invasion of the Egyptian mainland, essentially to regain control of the Suez Canal, and ensure continued safe navigation for international maritime trade, through this strategic waterway.

The minesweeping task was to clear the approaches to the canal at Port Said.

Intelligence had suggested, Egyptian Forces had access to sophisticated mines that, if deployed, would be a major threat to all craft approaching the entrance to the canal.

It was also obvious to us that minesweepers would be required to lead the landings, sweeping the approaches, thus safeguarding surface vessels carrying troops and equipment from such a threat.

Mines of Russian origin were extremely difficult to sweep, and we could expect casualties during clearance operations. Thankfully, the threat from mines did not materialize, and we sustained no casualties in that part of the operation.

Once the landings had been successfully completed, our tasks were more mundane, performing a variety of duties. It was necessary to recover the numerous Dan Buoy markers etc, laid to mark out the cleared approaches.

The main threat now, was sabotage. Having successfully secured the canal it was imperative to make sure it remained navigable, pending it's opening to normal traffic. For this duty the Minesweepers proved ideal.

Our size and draft allowed us to manoeuvre in the confined space of the canal, and we were able to patrol the area without difficulty, protecting equipment and installations from untoward attention

We were also available to Army units, for liaison purposes, as they continued southwards to consolidate the security of the area.

Militarily, Operation Musketeer appeared a success!

HMS Cavalier (Rtd)

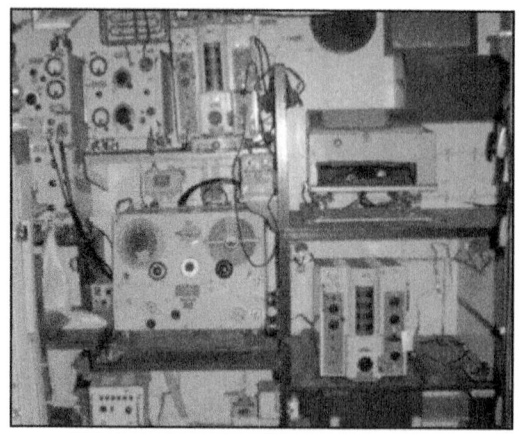

Heading towards retirement

Preserved at Chatham

Cavalier's Wireless Office.

"The communications branch is the finest in the Royal Navy which, in turn, is the finest service in the world".

Lord Louis Mountbatten

Appendix 5 — Memories Are Made Of This

HMS Cavalier (Rtd)

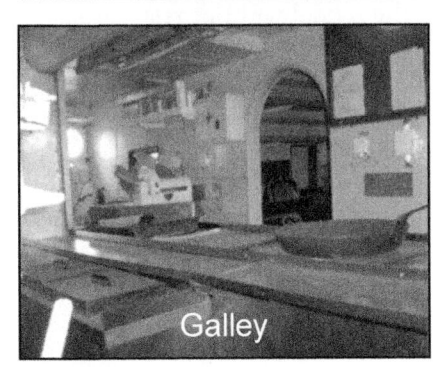

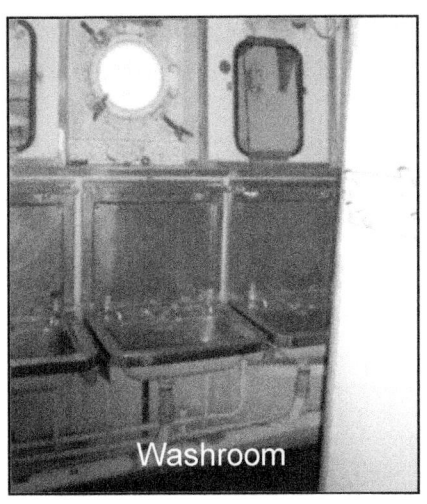

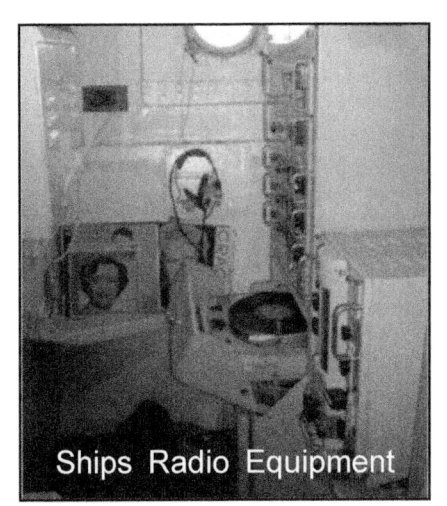

- Welcome aboard
- The Bridge
- View from the Bridge
- Galley
- The Rum Tub
- NAAFI
- Washroom
- Ships Radio Equipment
- Forward Head

Malaysian Medal

Pingat Jasa Malaysia (PJM) medal

"Pingat Jasa Malaysia" can be translated as "The Malaysian Service Medal". The medal was offered at the end of 2004 to the Commonwealth countries who served Malaysia in her fight against aggression and terrorism between the years 1956 to 1966. Those Commonwealth countries include Australia, New Zealand, Fiji, the United Kingdom and, never to be forgotten, the Gurkhas.

I applied for my Medal in early 2007, and I am still waiting. It would seem that a couple of Whitehall Civil Servants are trying to block the award of these Medals to the UK Veterans. However, knowing the power of persuasion of both Rum Ration and the Army unofficial Web site, ARSSE, I have every confidence that I will eventually receive mine along with the other 180,000 entitled Veterans.

Eventually received mine in May 2010.

The citation that accompanies the medal reads:

Pingat Jasa Malaysia

This medal is awarded to the peacekeeping groups amongst the Communion countries for distinguished chivalry, gallantry, sacrifice or loyalty in upholding Peninsula of Malaya or Malaysia sovereignty during the period of Emergency and Confrontation.

Foreign and Commonwealth medals have to be accepted by The Queen on the advice of the Government of each Commonwealth country involved where she is head of State. After a short period of consultation the Governments of Australia and New Zealand accepted the medal without restriction for their citizens. The British Government, however, announced in the House of Lords that they would refuse the Malaysian medal for British citizens on the basis that the award was contrary to British Medals Policy.

In early 2005 intensive lobbying commenced to try and reverse that decision and after a few months the Secretary of State at the Foreign and Commonwealth Office (FCO) announced that the FCO had submitted a paper to the Committee on the Grants of Honours, Decorations and Medals (known as the HD Committee which advises The Queen on these matters) asking them to review their policy in respect of foreign awards and the PJM.

The British HD Committee's recommendation, however, was that British citizens could accept the medal but they would not be allowed to wear it. This astonishing situation means that The Queen has granted a wearable medal to her Australian and New Zealand citizens, but has refused the right to wear the PJM to her British citizens.

Appendix 7 — Memories Are Made Of This

Maldive Islands

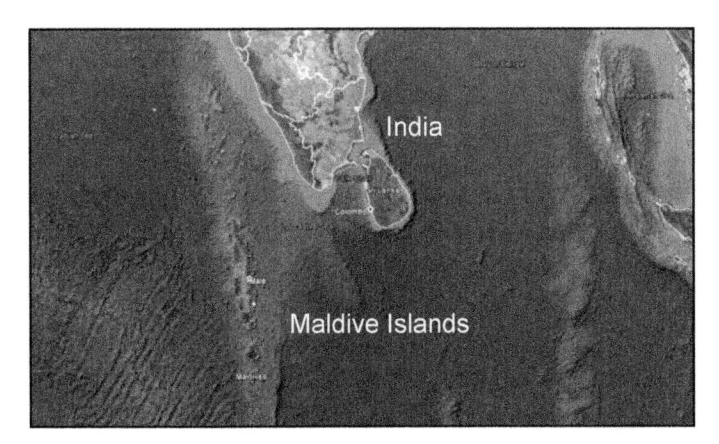

The Maldive Islands are an amazing spectacle, and I can well understand why they have now become so popular with tourists.

The highest point of land is only about two meters above sea level and, as you approach the islands, it looks as though there a palm trees growing out of the sea, and the land does not become apparent until you are almost on top of it.

When we were there, Costains were in the process of building a runway for RAF aircraft, and were thought to be threatened by the local natives who, at that time, were not exactly disposed towards westerners.

Our job was to anchor in the middle of the atoll, and discourage the natives from doing anything rash.

I think that we must have had a fair degree of influence on their thinking because, for the next month, we spent most of the time fishing, Bar B Queuing on the beach, watching evening film shows on board or enjoying the delights of the local Bar.

Anyway, as can be seen from the Google photographs, the runway did indeed get built and, as we gradually gave away the British Empire, the runway and facilities were handed over to the natives.

The Maldives are now being seriously threatened by rising seas due to global warning.

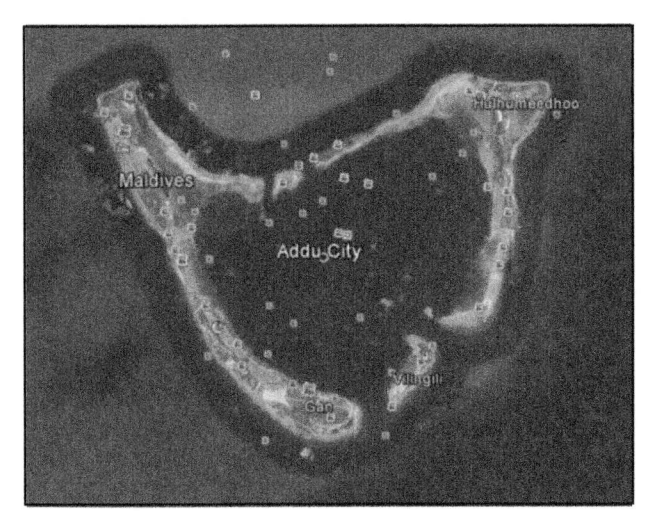

Appendix 8   Memories Are Made Of This

Royal Navy Retired

For my 70th birthday, my ex wife Joyce, daughter Susan and husband Pete, plus my two grand sons Ben and Mathew, treated me to a day out at Chatham Dockyard to visit Cavalier. What I had not realised was that, besides being my birthday, it was also separate anniversaries for both Cavalier and Chatham Dockyard, and, between all of them, they had organised and laid on a very special day for me.

The first that I knew about it was when we were greeted our tour guide for the day, Scot, dressed as a Pirate, who presented me with a book and a Compliment slip signed by the Admiral. I have to say that both the family and Chatham did me proud, and it was quite an emotional day.

Naval Humour

A collection of Humour in Uniform, trawled from various sites on the Internet. And, whereas I cannot vouch for their veracity, my past experience leads me to believe that they all possess a grain of truth.

Matelot bumbling across Horse Guards Parade, passes a Guards officer but fails to salute.
Guards officer: "Don't you salute Army officers in the Navy?"
Matelot: "We haven't got any Army officers in the Navy!"

A Wren sees the Admiral, with a piece of paper in his hand, standing by the classified document shredder.
Admiral: "Do you know how to work this thing? My Secretary has left for the day, and I have no idea how to run it".
Wren: "Yes sir".
She turns on the machine, takes the paper from the Admiral and feeds it in.
Admiral: "Thank you, I only need one copy".

Captain; "Paint on my hands again Number One".
1st Lieutenant: "Where from sir?"
Captain: "Bridge ladder, Number One".
1st Lieutenant: "But the bridge ladder has not been painted for three months sir".
Captain: "Why not?"
1st Lieutenant "Er, yes sir".

OOW: "I say Lookout, what do you estimate the range of visibility to be?".
Lookout: "About ninety three million miles sir, I can see the Sun".
OOW: "Ah yes, I suppose I asked for that. Droll, very droll".

Army officer approaches and, true to the Naval Tradition of "No Saluting indoors", our hero's nod as they pass each other.
Army officer: "Don't you Navy Types compliment an Officer when passing".
Navy Types: "Oh, sorry sir. Nice trousers", and wend their way to the Bar.

Sparks was on the helm of a Submarine, when the Officer on the Conning Tower screams down the voice pipe,
"Who is the thick sh*t on the end of this voice pipe?".
Sparks: "Which end sir?".

'Never let the truth spoil a good Dit'
Navy Anon

Appendix 9 — Memories Are Made Of This

Naval Humour

"Julian, You were only supposed To blow the bloody Doors off!"

DANGER! UNEXPLODED AMMUNITION

Suez

"Gentlemen, welcome to my first Ann Summers party".

Naval Humour

Quotations contributed, compiled and cobbled together by the complement and crew of Rum Ration, and now preserved for posterity. For more of the same, visit the Rum Ration site.

On Joining

When I joined The Navy I wanted to be a cook, but they already had one.

If you're looking for sympathy, you'll find it in the dictionary, between shit and syphilis.

When I joined the Navy, we didn't get Identity Cards, we all knew each other.

On The Morning After

Woke up with a mouth like the bottom of Cairo crab catchers worm bag.

Mouth like Gandhi's port and starboard flip flops!

On The Useless

He can calculate the circumference and cubic capacity of an orange, just don't ask him to peel it.

He never makes the same mistake twice. However.....

You've got as much chance as striking a match on wet tripe!

As useless as an ashtray on a motorbike.

Couldn't organize 50% leave in a two man submarine.

Couldn't organise a piss up in a Brewery.

About as useful as a fart in a fan shaft.

On Length Of Service

I was in the Navy when the Dead Sea reported sick.

I knew Pontius Pilot when he was an Air Cadet.

I was in uniform when you were in liquid form.

I joined up when the Mary Rose was still in Epping forest.

I was only interested in the raising of the Mary Rose because I thought I might recover my kit bag.

On Ugly Women

She's got a face like a bulldog chewing a wasp.

She had a face like a badly packed kit bag.

She had a face like a dockyard welders bench.

How can you be so ugly with only one head?

Everybody has the right to be ugly but she abuses the privilege.

Never been to bed with an ugly woman, but sure woke up with few.

She had teeth like a NAAFI piano keyboard, one white, one black, one missing.

On Obese Women

She was so fat she had to fart to give me a clue.

Naval Humour.

I found this on the Ganges web site. It rang so many bells that I just had to include it:

Author: **Capt. George F. Morgan RAMC (Rtd)**

The year was 1958, aged 14, my friend Roger Grant and I were Ramsgate Sea Cadet's recently returned from a two week summer course in Seamanship at HMS Ganges. A major annual event in the Royal Navy is Navy Days held at the various H M Dockyards. H M Dockyard Chatham was but a short one and a quarter hour train ride from Broadstairs and as Sea Cadets, so long as we were in uniform, we were permitted free entry.

The quiet still of a summer morning was suddenly bought back to reality by the sound of a Bosun's whistle playing the Still immediately followed by the bellowing sound of the Provost Bosun's Mate standing full square in the centre of the Main Gate, feet astride, and fists on hips. "Put your bloody caps on straight, get your cuffs buttoned and double your arses over here… NOW! I said double you scruffy swabs."

As fast as our trembling fingers could manage we fumbled with our cuff buttons, squared our caps away and doubled to the gate. Standing now to attention in front of a PO bearing a NP armband (Naval Police) he seemed to me to be the biggest Policeman I had ever seen. We were turned to the left and marched into the Guard Room at double, double time. The dressing down that we received that morning was long and full of adjectives the like of which I had never heard before strung together, as they were, into a number of long sentences all of which ended in the exclamation of "Got It!?":

"I am Petty Officer Snudgit Bleedin' Bligh – Got It!"

"Yessssssssssss"

"Shut it, no one asked for a speech from Yooo – Got It!"
"Related I is to Capt. Bligh of HMS Bounty – Got It!"
"I could 'ave you lashed to the mast – Got It!"
"Oh yes, I likes a good floggin, me! – Got It!"
"Duty Provost of HMS bleedin' Pembroke is what I is – Got It!"
"I makes sure, little swabbies like what you is do things right – Got It!"
"Crabby little swabbies like you two do not abuse the Queen's Uniform – Got It!"
"Ow did you abuse the Queen's, God bless 'er, uniform swabby?"

"Please Sir, we…."

"Shut up, ooo asked you to speak, you don't speak until your told – Got It!"
"Orrible little swabbies like you do not meander down my Dock Road – Got It!"
"Orrible little swabbies like you March in a smart and sailor like fashion down my Dock Road – Got It!"

"Move to the right in line, RIGHT TURN, double MARCH, left, right, left right, left wheel, right wheel, mark time, HALT".

"Wot we ave ere, my Crabby little Swabbies is the Provost's Galley – Got It!"
"Shut It!"
"And by all that's glorious in this man's navy; just look wot we got ere – lots-n-lots of dirty breakfast dishes."

Printed in Great Britain
by Amazon